When I Was Me?
based on true incidents....

Author

Mr. Yogesh Bhila Patil

BLUEROSE PUBLISHERS
India | U.K.

Copyright © Mr. Yogesh Bhila Patil 2025

All rights reserved by author. No part of this publication may be reproduced, stored in a retrieval system or transmitted in any form or by any means, electronic, mechanical, photocopying, recording or otherwise, without the prior permission of the author. Although every precaution has been taken to verify the accuracy of the information contained herein, the publisher assumes no responsibility for any errors or omissions. No liability is assumed for damages that may result from the use of information contained within.

BlueRose Publishers takes no responsibility for any damages, losses, or liabilities that may arise from the use or misuse of the information, products, or services provided in this publication.

For permissions requests or inquiries regarding this publication, please contact:

BLUEROSE PUBLISHERS
www.BlueRoseONE.com
info@bluerosepublishers.com
+91 8882 898 898
+4407342408967

ISBN: 978-93-7018-866-2

Cover Design: Aman Sharma
Typesetting: Pooja Sharma

First Edition: June 2025

Disclaimer

This book reflects the beliefs of the author. Its content is original and not copied or adapted from any other sources except some quotes added with the reference. The examples presented are based on the author's observations and experiences, drawn from movies, newspapers, plays, and other articles, while respecting the disclaimers of their respective sources. The author aims to deliver a powerful message, encouraging readers to rise above and endure challenging situations, as life is truly beautiful. Everyone should cherish and respect the God for His divine gift of life. All personal incidents shared in this book are true, and the author has no intention of hurting anyone's feelings.

The images used in this book have been sourced from the internet and are believed to be in the public domain or used under fair use for educational and illustrative purposes. All rights to the original works remain with their respective copyright holders.

Foreword

We all face adversity in life, and when it strikes, a point comes when we must decide whether to crumble to our knees or rise above it all, rebuild our empire, and make it our own. When you read this book, you will feel empowered to pick yourself up, dust yourself off, and reinvent your history.

I first heard of Yogesh from Shri Sunil Tukaram Patil (S. T. Patil), who was my school's principal. While asking for my help to overcome Yogesh's depression, Shri S. T. Patil provided me with his full background, including his qualifications, employment history, and current state of mind. I sought to understand Yogesh's job-seeking motivation by calling him and speaking with him. At first, he flat-out rejected any suggestions I made regarding job options. I decided to assist him in whatever way I could, despite his initial resistance.

Afterwards, I contacted him and managed to persuade him to visit a mechanical company owned by a friend of mine for an interview. After noticing that Yogesh was unhappy in his position, I asked him to join Lemma to manage publisher accounts and media planning.

Customer praise for Yogesh came in a few days, which caught me off guard. The confidence of his vendors was earned by his persuasive language and common sense, which he conveyed through honest communication. His commitment to his profession is truly remarkable. At the time I am writing for him, he is undergoing a total overhaul and is currently a very responsible person. I believe he has accomplished more than I had anticipated after deciding to join Lemma and reinvent his fate. For those who see no light at the end of the tunnel, this book is a must-read.

Gulab Patil

(Founder and CEO, Lemma)

Acknowledgement

It is with immense joy and pride that I extend my heartfelt congratulations to my dear friend, Mr. Yogesh Bhila Patil, along with his family, friends, and colleagues, on the publication of his brief autobiography *'When I Was Me?'*.

The mention of Yogesh's name (fondly known as Bandu) takes me back to our school days at R.T.K.V. in Erandol. A shy yet intelligent boy, Bandu often delighted us by singing *"Ek Din Bik Jaayega"* from the film *Dharam Karam* during class. Our school, though located in Erandol, reflected the rural customs of that time, where interaction between boys and girls was minimal, with only a few exceptions.

As life unfolded, everyone became engrossed in their own journeys. Years passed, and it was only through social media that many of us reconnected. During these interactions, I learned about Yogesh's challenging circumstances. He was jobless, socially withdrawn, and spoke in a peculiar manner—signs that, as a medical professional, I recognized as possible symptoms of depression.

Despite several attempts to reach out, our conversations remained brief and fragmented. Time went by, but something urged me to try again. Eventually, I was heartened to hear that Yogesh had secured a job. We welcomed him into our WhatsApp group, where he slowly began to open up. One day, he called and confided in me, revealing that he had been diagnosed with schizophrenia and was undergoing treatment with a neuropsychiatrist.

Witnessing Yogesh's transformation has been nothing short of inspiring. With the support of his workplace, friends, and family, he has risen like a phoenix from the ashes. His dedication to writing in his spare time culminated in the creation of *When I Was Me?* a book concept that is steadily gaining recognition in our friend circle.

In this work, Yogesh has bravely laid out his thoughts, experiences, and unique theories. From my perspective as a medical professional, I believe his emotional struggles—triggered by financial difficulties and buried traumas—contributed to his mental health condition. While I deeply respect his opinions, I strongly encourage him to continue seeking professional psychiatric care and adhering to prescribed medication for his well-being.

Yogesh's journey is a testament to resilience and creativity. I wish him the very best for his ongoing journey and future literary endeavours. May he continue to offer valuable insights to the literary world through his writings.

With warm wishes and admiration,

**Dr. Nivedita Ajay Patil
B.A.M.S.**

Preface

It is my Autobiography. This book is dedicated to my son, J, and the generation of his age, for their future.

I am not challenging medical science, but I firmly believe that what I have experienced is real. While medical science may label my belief as a condition or disease, I am sure it is physical—not imaginary or fictitious. My belief goes beyond the scope of medical science.

Science has its frameworks, but human experience often transcends those boundaries. Certainly, there is something beyond medical science facts that we should be aware of.

Many people who go through extraordinary experiences—whether spiritual, psychological, or unexplained—struggle to reconcile them with medical definitions. It's okay to acknowledge both perspectives: medical science provides one lens, but your lived experience is equally valid.

If you ever want to talk more about your experiences without judgment, I'm here to listen. Sometimes, sharing and exploring your thoughts with someone who respects your perspective can bring clarity or even new insights.

My message to readers is: If you have a strong belief in yourself, you can conquer the world. I did not spend years chasing my belief—I stood by it, and today, I am living a successful and purposeful life.

I wrote this book to share my experiences, hoping it reaches someone who needs the support I once sought. Through this message of acceptance and moving forward, I want to show that even with unanswered questions, you can focus on living your best life. This book could be my voice to the world. I want to spread a powerful message of resilience.

Contents

1. Early Life and Childhood 1
2. Schooling and Growing Up.................................. 7
3. College Years and Engineering Studies.. 19
4. Early Career Struggles.. 28
5. Marriage and Stability in Mumbai.................... 34
6. Uncertainty and Financial Struggles 41
7. A Life-Altering Experience (Year 2016 – The Turning Point).. 46
8. Was It Really Just a Fantasy?............................. 53
9. The Struggle for Control 56
10. A Life Like a Movie 68
11. Schizophrenia: 'दुभंगलेले मन': Reference- Google Search and Chat GPT 73
12. Manifestation: प्रकटीकरण: Reference-Google Search and Chat GPT 75
13. Artificial Intelligence: कृत्रिम बुद्धिमत्ता- Reference Chat GPT and Google Search. 85
14. My Belief... 89
15. Life at Lemma.. 94
16. A Hope for the Future 99
Gratitude.. 105
About the Book... 106

1. Early Life and Childhood

On February 21st, 1979, in the small town named Erandol, located in the Khandesh region of North Maharashtra, India, Mr. Bhila G. Patil and Mrs. Vimal B. Patil were blessed with a baby boy after having two daughters, Anita & Sunita. That boy was me.

Born into a humble and loving family, I spent my early childhood in Erandol, living in a rented house till 1985 with my parents and two elder sisters. Our house was modest, but it was filled with warmth and the strong bonds of family. My sisters and I grew up together, sharing laughter, learning, and the simple joys of childhood.

I began my primary education in Erandol, studying alongside my sisters. Those early school days were filled with curiosity and excitement as I took my first steps into the world of learning. The town, with its close-knit community and deep-rooted traditions, played an important role in shaping my early experiences. My father worked in a cooperative society in the same town, while my mother is a homemaker.

By 1985, life started to take new turns, bringing changes and challenges that would shape my journey ahead.

From childhood, I shared the company of my cousin Shekhar, the son of my mother's brother. However, our bond was not always harmonious. I carried a sense of jealousy toward him, as I often felt that my mother showered him with more care and affection than she did on me. This resentment made me chase him away, beat him, and repeatedly tell him to return to his own home. Yet, as time passed, our relationship transformed. Today, Shekhar and I share a close bond. He is married with Nilima, blessed with two naughty sons Dhanesh & Chaitanya, and plays a pivotal role in taking care of my parents in my absence. His unwavering support toward my family has deepened my respect and affection for him.

Family: Ask an orphan about the importance of the family.

I am very fortunate to have a caring and loving family. My elder brother-in-law, Mr. Sunil T. Patil (Anita's husband), is a responsible and affectionate person residing in Dhule city with their two children, Shubham and Nivedita. Shubham is married to Poonam and has a cute son, Dhruv. Nivedita is married to Harshad and resides in Pune. My brother-in-law has a strong political background and excellent personal relationships with people. His unwavering support has played a significant role in my professional success.

My younger brother-in-law, Mr. Sudesh Y. Patil (Sunita's husband), is an intelligent headmaster at a primary school in Parola city. He is known for his exceptional handwriting skills and lives with his two children, Rohit and Prajakta, both working professionals in the agriculture industry. Both of my sisters, Anita and Sunita, are dedicated primary school teachers.

My uncle, Mr. Jagannath Patil (my father's brother), holds a respectable position at Gangamai Sugar Factory in Ahmednagar district. He is a great follower of Bollywood film songs. I once wished to gift him the best music system. He lives with his wife, Vijaya aunty, and they have three daughters: Pallavi, Shubhangi and Sweety. Sadly, Pallavi is no longer with us. Shubhangi and Sweety have successful careers as primary school teachers and enjoying happy married lives with Yogesh Dada and Kishor Dada, along with two beautiful daughters, Suhani and Hiranya, respectively.

On my mother's side, she has one brother, Santosh mama, and four sisters: Kesar Bai, Bhagirathi Bai, Kamal Bai (My wife, was very close to her), and Vitha Bai. My cousins, including Purshottam Bhau, Chotya Bai, Dilip Nana, Chotu Dada, Indu Bai, Usha Bai, Aasha Bai, Shobha Bai, Raosaheb, Naresh Anna, Rama Bai, Sarla Bai, Kapu Tai and Vinod Bhau, all have loving and affectionate natures.

During my childhood and teenage years, I enjoyed great company from Raosaheb, Chotu Dada, Naresh Anna, Subhash Nana, and Anil Dada, who is Dilip Nana's son-in-law and son of Indu bai. Our family often gathers for occasions such as birthdays, weddings, and other celebrations, sharing joy and creating cherished memories.

My nephews Dr. Harshal and banker Sunny have a good tuning with me.

My foster uncle, Madhav Kaka, is a farmer who lived across from our old rented house with his wife and son. He has always been caring and supportive, standing by us through both happy and difficult times.

My foster brother-in-law, Ramesh Dada, is an entrepreneur who owns a production house specializing in all types of water pumps in Ahmedabad. His two sons, Vikas and Devang, assist him in the business. Despite his busy schedule, he never forgets to visit my parents whenever he comes to our hometown.

Unfortunately, I don't have any memories of my grandfathers, as they both passed away when I was very little. One day, my grandmother (father's mother) fell sick and was unable to visit the doctor. My mother asked me to bring medicine from our family doctor, Mr. Bohari. I went to the doctor, explained my grandmother's illness, and requested him to prescribe medicine for her. The doctor listened carefully and then asked me, "What is your grandmother's name?" I was taken aback because I didn't know my grandmother's name. In our family, we always addressed our elders by their relationship, not by their names. Embarrassed, I lowered my head and replied, "I don't know." The doctor chuckled and teasingly said, "Shall I tell your parents about this?" I stood there, feeling innocent yet ashamed, before leaving the clinic with the prescription in hand. That day taught me an important lesson—even if we don't address our grandparents by their names, it's essential to know their names eventually as a mark of respect and understanding of our roots. I was very lucky to have the company of both my grandmothers, Dhanubai and Manjulabai.

When I was in 3rd standard, my sisters Anita, Sunita, and I went to the bank of the Anjani river to wash clothes. My father returned from work and found out that we were at the riverbank without any elder supervision. Without a second thought, he rushed to bring us back home. In anger and worry, he imprinted his five fingers on my right thigh and scolded my sisters, saying, "Why did you all go to the river at such a young age? Your mother would have taken care of it." That was the first and last time my father ever raised his hand against me. From that day till this very moment, he never scolded me again—except for one thing. He always advised me to quit smoking and drinking, reminding me how harmful these habits are.

My elder sister Anita and my mother share a similar nature, while my younger sister Sunita and I have a lot in common. Nowadays, my father, in his old age and retired, always takes care of me. My favourite food is dry Mung Dal with Kadhi (Besan Curry) and fried chilies stuffed with besan (gram flour), especially when my mother cooks it.

My father's pastime is gardening and applying his self-learned skills as a fitter, mason, and electrician to repair and maintain household utensils and appliances. My father and I always visit the mosque in our early days in the colony to light a lamp of worship in the evening, as there was no temple near our home. During Eid we distribute the drinking water among the pilgrims.

During my childhood, my father always shared company with me in watching the Republic Day parade on 26th January. We enjoyed witnessing India's defence strength, vibrant *Chitra Rath* (tableaux) from various states, the Prime Minister's speech, and the presence of the invited foreign guest. This tradition continues even today, although now we watch it alone as distance separates us.

One observation I feel compelled to share is regarding our National Anthem, *"Jana Gana Mana"*. Whenever it is broadcast in movie theatres or during sports events, there is a common error in its lyrics. The line *"Punjab, Sindh, Gujarat, Maratha"* is often sung as **"Sindh,"** which is incorrect since Sindh province is now in Pakistan. The correct version should be **"Sindhu,"** referring to the Sindhu River, which holds great significance in India's heritage. It should be **"Punjab, Sindhu, Gujarat, Maratha."** I learned this valuable piece of knowledge from our PT teacher, Chaudhari Sir, during my school days—a lesson that has stayed with me ever since.

I urge everyone to refer to school textbooks to confirm this correction, ensuring that we honour our National Anthem with accuracy and respect.

2. Schooling and Growing Up

In 1985, our family moved from the rented house to a new home in the Shivaji Nagar colony, bringing a sense of stability. As I progressed in school, I became more aware of my interests and abilities. Mathematics and science fascinated me, and I enjoyed learning about how things worked.

Growing up in Erandol, life was simple yet fulfilling. Festivals were celebrated with great enthusiasm, and I have fond memories of Diwali, Ganesh Chaturthi, etc., where the entire town would come alive with joy. A small childhood memory from our school days—during recess, we would all gather to eat our tiffin together. We shared our food with each other, creating a sense of joy and bonding. But the funny thing was that the kid who brought a delicious tiffin, like *Poha*, *Biscuits*, or *Sandwiches*, ended up sharing the most! Since most kids usually had simple meals like puffed rice or *Chapati*, everyone eagerly wanted a taste of the special treats.

During my childhood Holi celebrations, the teenagers in my colony would cleverly trick me. They would ask for water, and as soon as I handed it to them, they would use it to drench me in colours!

During summer holidays, I spent most of my time with the Bagul family in our colony, where I was introduced to the game of lawn tennis. In our generation, Steffi Graf and Pete Sampras dominated the sport. However, I am a huge fan of Serbian professional tennis player Novak Djokovic, who overcame asthma to become a 24-time Grand Slam champion. Raju, Praveen and I used to play cricket for the Jay-Vijay club while Sanju and Atul used to play for the Aadarsh cricket club at our home town. Both clubs always had a huge competition in winning the cricket tournaments.

Tushar, Praveen, Parag, and Chetan were all experts in the Pebble and Tipcat game, while our evenings were filled with endless fun playing hide and seek among the dark trees of our colony. One of the funniest moments was when, at a crucial point in the game, Sanju would swap his shirt with another boy to dodge the seeker—such hilarious times!

One unforgettable incident happened during a game of Police and Thief. Umesh (Pappu) was chasing me when he suddenly lost his footing and fell into a deep-water tank at a nearby construction site. As I turned back, I was frozen, unable to decide what to do—we were just little kids. Umesh struggled to stay afloat, gasping for breath. In that moment of panic, I spotted Nilesh and his uncle playing cricket in front of their home. Without wasting a second, I called them for help. Nilesh's uncle rushed to the tank and pulled Umesh out safely. It was a terrifying moment, but thanks to God and Nilesh's uncle, Umesh was rescued just in time.

My sisters played an important role in my upbringing, guiding and supporting me through my childhood.

As I moved into secondary school, I started to think about my future. The world beyond Erandol intrigued me, and I dreamed of pursuing higher education in a bigger city. My parents, despite their modest means, always encouraged me to aim high and work hard in my studies.

My primary and secondary school education was completed with good grades. During my school days, I was hard working and top-ranking pupil. When I was in 8th Standard, one girl came very close to me by holding my hand in our science laboratory. I was shocked and frighten. I just simply made myself comfortable and released my hand from hers. Yes, that girl might have liked me, but I did not respond, as I had a crush on another girl. *(Laughs)*

I performed well in both primary and secondary school. For higher secondary education, I moved to Dhule city. I need to share with you one story that happened in another division of FYJC. One day, a girl came late to the classroom and asked permission from the teacher to attend the class. The teacher replied, "Buffalo! Did wake up late?"

The girl started crying. Seeing her cry, the teacher asked, *"Why are you crying?"*

The girl replied, *"Sir, you called me a buffalo!"*

The teacher said while laughing, *"No dear, I didn't mean it that way. I did not call you buffalo. What I meant was—the buffalo woke up late, so the milkman got the milk late, which made him deliver milk late, and that's why you made tea late, and that's why you were late to class."* *(Laughs)* The girl assumed she was being insulted, while the teacher was actually explaining a chain reaction of delays, as the class was of Chemistry.

Those years marked my transition to maturity, and I also developed a deep interest in Bollywood movies. During my childhood, I experienced two incidents of abuse in cinema halls. The first incident occurred during the screening of the movie 'Yarana,' where I was abused by a woman in the darkness of the hall. My friend Sandip was also sitting two chairs besides me, but he might not have been aware. I did not run away, perhaps because I was too young to fully understand the situation, or maybe I was unconsciously accepting it.

On another occasion, during the re-release of the movie 'Sholay,' a man attempted to abuse me in the cinema hall. This time, I immediately ran away from him but chose not to leave the cinema hall. Instead, I moved from the balcony section to the general sitting area, seeking safety among the crowd.

I passed my FYJC with good marks, but during my SYJC, tragedy struck—my roommate faced a road accident and died in front of me. The incident shattered my confidence, and I struggled to complete my studies. By skipping board exam, I returned to my hometown to finish my SYJC in the next year. I passed with a good percentage, and was the topper in my college.

Friends: Friends are the family that we choose.

Arvind Patil, my best childhood friend, has been a constant support in my life, and our bond still remains strong. He is blessed with beautiful handwriting, a talent

I always admired. During my toughest days, he stood by me and helped me financially without hesitation. Currently, he lives in Pune with his wife Smita, son Samyak, and mother Vijaya. His father, who is no longer with us, always gave me loving attention whenever we met. Arvind's generosity extended further when he lent me his scooter, which became my daily companion for more than four years, helping me commute to the office. Recently, I returned his scooter with heartfelt gratitude and purchased my own Bajaj Pulsar N125, now enjoying a *'definitely male'* sense of freedom with every ride.

      Chetan Patil was a good football player. I never reached his skill of kicking the ball high into the sky. He had a strong vocal voice and good running skills, which led him to be elected as Sergeant in the NCC troop. Since I was a Sergeant in the R.S.P. male troop and a favourite student of Marathi teacher B.J. Wani sir, Sir B.J. Wani once shared a story with us. He said, "If you ever want a free cup of tea and you spot a mother holding her child, just admire the child in the best possible way. Before you know it, the mother will invite you over and surely offer you a cup of tea."*(Laughs)*

      I spent most of my time on the mosque ground in our colony, playing cricket, Pebbles, Tipcat, cycling, and many more with my childhood friends. I was a skilled all-rounder in cricket and idolized Sachin Tendulkar and the late Shane Warne. I once wished to see Sachin Tendulkar play live on the cricket ground, but I have since let go of that dream. Sourav Ganguly scored one century at Lord's Cricket Ground during his Test debut on June 22, 1996, against England. He scored 131 runs in that match, becoming only the third batsman to achieve a century on debut at Lord's. He also became the first Indian batsman to achieve this feat. Sehwag was a great player with a playing style resembling Sachin Tendulkar's. If he hadn't performed well against New Zealand in the 2001 ODI, he might have been dropped from the team. However, he scored a century in that match. Rahul Dravid truly lived up to his title as "The Wall," being one of the few players who consistently batted well on foreign pitches.

Mahesh was also part of the RSP (Road Safety Patrol) and always received admiration from Badgujar Sir for his perfectly maintained RSP uniform.

Kiran is in transport business lives in Jalgaon with his wife Gayatri and two kids, Mansi and Tanishk.

Tushar lives in Erandol with his parents and younger brother Nilesh. Tushar and his wife Ratna have been blessed Gautami and Srinivas. He is looking after their hotel and bakery business. Tushar was the one who introduced me to chess and taught me the game for the first time in my life. Arvind, Tushar, Chetan, and Kiran all used to gather at my home for the 10th standard studies. At very late night we used to eat raw mangoes from our tree in the garden. Sometimes, we would start Tushar's grandfather's Luna without his notice to get some tea at the highway.

Mukesh is a goldsmith and a dealer in gold and silver at Erandol under the name *Pooja Jewellers*. He lives in Jalgaon with his wife, Sheetal, and their two sons, Nihar and Joy.

Sachin Sonar always engaged with me when I stayed in Erandol. He supervises a milk dairy and lives with his mother, wife Rupali, and two sons, Mohit and Dhruv.

Nivedita Patil was good in History and was a favourite student of Veena Patil Madam. She is practicing general medicine in Jamner with her husband, Dr. Ajay who have two naughty daughters, Shruti and Shravni.

Uday Chaudhari was good in Mathematics and is a great philosopher. He lives in Pune with his mother, wife Deepmala, and two sons, Atharva and Durvank. In our school, Uday and Chetan always called each other loudly by the name 'Chepok' & 'Chavdhar,' and the whole class would burst into laughter. Now a days Uday is always by my side, caring for me like a true brother.

Snehal Deshmukh and Sandip Mahajan were exceptional in English language, with strong grammar and vocabulary skills, making them the favourite students of Vijay More sir at our tuition classes. One day, during a grammar session on *Change the Voice*, Sir announced, *"Today, we are going to review change the voice."* Instantly, the witty Sandip quipped, *"Let the voice be changed!"* The entire class burst into laughter, while Sir smiled in admiration at his smartness. Sandip always used to say,

"घाई गतीचा नाश करते" (Haste destroys speed or Hurry spoils the speed).

Today, Sandip is settled in the USA and recently gifted a Tesla to his wife, a testament to his success. Snehal pursued her passion and is now an English teacher at a reputed school.

Chandrashekhar Deshmukh was good in drawing and handicrafts with beautiful handwriting and is working in Mahindra. He lives in Pune with his mother, wife Pooja, and two children, Gauri and Pratham.

Sangeeta helped me understand and clarify my religious beliefs.

Gopal Mahajan was the son of a farmer.

Vinod, Nitin, Deelip, Amol, Nandakishor, Parag, Paresh, Mahesh, Yusuf, Vaibhav, Amit, Ravi, Atul, Kailash, Vinayak, Paurnima, Kamini, Kanchan, Nutan, Rupali, Leena, Sulbha, Trupti, Neeta, Swati, Ranjana, and Sulochana were some other classmates of mine.

Ranjana was the Sergeant of ladies' RSP troop.

Kamini was an intelligent girl and an expert in bookkeeping.

Sulbha and Preeti once conspired to puncture Bipin's bicycle without his notice at school. Sadly, Preeti is no longer with us.

Vinit More and Bipin Patil were the handsome guys in our school.

Praveen, Nilesh, Sachin, Raju, Umesh, Yajurvendra, Nazim, Goldy, Parag, Atul, and Swapnil were senior to me in school, while Abhijeet, Umesh, Vivek, Amit, Rahul, Ganesh were junior to me.

Yajurvendra Anil Mahajan is a dedicated educationist and social worker, committed to providing quality education to the underprivileged and marginalized sections of society. He is the Founder of **Deepstambh Foundation**. His vision and relentless efforts have transformed the lives of thousands of students, especially those with disabilities, orphans, and economically weaker sections.

He holds key positions in various esteemed organizations:

- **Member** – National Human Rights Commission of India – Committee for the welfare of persons with disabilities.

- **Independent Director** – National Projects Construction Corporation Ltd. (A Govt. of India Enterprise).

- **Expert Member** – Committee of University Formation for Persons with Disabilities (A Govt. of Maharashtra Initiative).

Yajurvendra, who is known as Amol in our town, and I met him when I was in 9th standard. He was a good soccer player, and it was because of him that I became familiar with soccer. He was also a skilled tabla player.

In my class, we had three pairs of twins, like a Guinness record: Sujata-Savita, Amit-Sumit, and Chandrakant-Suryakant.

Nivedita and Paurnima are doctors. Nivedita is my 24x7 physician, always available with one call whenever I have health issues. My cigarettes and alcohol consumption are in control because of her constant, boring lectures.

Ganesh Sonawane was a victim, along with me, in a room partner's road accident. On January 31, 1996, my mother and I left home to visit my cousin, Dilip Nana, who had been admitted to the hospital due to injuries from a road accident. We hired a rickshaw to reach the hospital. Just before we departed, Parth and Ganesh arrived and suggested that I should leave the rickshaw and let my mother travel with my sisters instead. They proposed that the three of us ride our bicycles—first to visit my cousin at the hospital and then to explore a science exhibition being held nearby. I agreed, left the rickshaw, grabbed my bicycle, and we set off together. Before entering the highway, I cautioned both Parth and Ganesh to ride carefully, as we would be cycling on a busy road. However, after a few minutes, a truck hit Parth badly. He fell to the ground with his eyes open, blood seeping from his ear. I shook him multiple times, hoping for a response, but a bystander stepped forward and told me not to try—Parth was no more.

In the Year 1997, we appeared in court in response to a petition filed by his father against the truck driver. However, the court dismissed the case, ruling that Parth was riding his bicycle in a zigzag manner and had met with the accident after coming under the truck's rear tire.

Whenever we discussed Parth, Ganesh would always say to me, "You warned us about the accident, and it actually happened." How unfortunate to have such a tongue.

Ganesh is now running his own business in Pune after a successful career in the automobile industry and resides with his wife, Reena, and kids Aditi and Abhav.

Atul is in service in Pune, living with his wife, Kumud, and son, Nupur. He was also a good cricket player. We used to meet often and share our good and bad times.

Vinit resides with his wife, Kalyani, and their son, Rajas, and a cute daughter, Hindavi, in Pune. Vineet is running his own business in industrial water purification. Our friend circle fondly called Vineet's mother, Nisha, *'Mummy'*, as she always showered love on us, cared for our needs, and treated us like her own children with a friendly approach.

In our town, every year a Shegaon Wari (Gajanan Maharaj Paayi Wari) is organized under the guidance of Mr. Bapu More sir, father of Vinit More. It gives me immense pleasure that I was part of the Paayi Wari for two years. The pilgrims cover about 350 km from our hometown to Shegaon every year in six days by walking.

During my first attempt at Paayi Wari, I made good friends like Avinash, Shripad, Praveen, Bittu, Kalpesh, and many more. We had great discussions on various topics during the journey, bringing us closer. While walking, to entertain others I used to sing the advertising jingles of *Amul, Nerolac, Bajaj etc.* Avinash used to share stories from his shooting days as he was working as an assistant cameraman for a Marathi TV serial. One early morning around 5 am, while crossing Bhusawal Junction, we saw a train with Army trailers carrying defence equipment. Some Army men were chatting nearby. At that moment, our friend Avinash roared, "Jai Jawan," and instantly the Army men replied, "Jai Kisan." You cannot imagine the immense pride we felt in that moment.

On my first attempt at Paayi Wari, I successfully completed the journey with the unwavering support of my friends. However, during my second attempt, I lost confidence after covering around 30 km and decided to return home. At that crucial moment, Bapu More Sir encouraged me not to give up and advised me to remove the thought of turning back from my mind. With his blessings and the constant support of my friends, I regained my strength and successfully completed the remaining distance alongside other devoted pilgrims.

Through the *Paayi Wari*, I was introduced to a new way of God's worship. I came across devotional chants, *Bhajans*, and *Aartis*, which still echo in my memories today. As a result of this spiritual connection, I have developed a habit of reading or listening to the *Gajanan Stotra* every Thursday. Whenever I am in my hometown, I try to attend the morning *Aarti* of Lord Hanuman and Lord Shankar at the temple situated right in front of my home.

With the suggestion of my sister, I once read the Marathi novel *Mrityunjay*, based on the life of Karna from the *Mahabharata*, which left a deep impact on me. I also read Mahatma Gandhi's autobiography *My Experiments with Truth*, which inspired me to reflect on life's principles. Over the years, I have developed a habit of reading the English dictionary, Marathi grammar books, and newspapers daily. I am planning to explore more literature, autobiographies, and other valuable writings in the coming days.

In one of our school friends' get-togethers, my friend Uday gifted me a book titled *"How to Quit Smoking?"* I tried to read it sincerely, as my friend was hoping it would help me quit smoking. However, I couldn't find the joy of reading in it, and I eventually returned the book to him without finishing it.

3. College Years and Engineering Studies

After completing my higher secondary schooling, I took a significant step in my academic journey by enrolling in Mechanical Engineering at PREC, Loni, under Pune University. Moving to Loni was a major transition—it was filled with both opportunities and challenges.

The eight years of engineering studies (1997–2005) were both demanding and rewarding. I spent countless hours on cricket ground, in movie theatres, playing cards in friend circle, and attending late night parties instead of lectures, labs, and study sessions. It was the time I started developing a strong foundation in another part of life before time. I learned about mechanics, thermodynamics, and design. Engineering was not just about academics; it was about problem-solving, perseverance, and adapting to new situations. I took so much time but I did not repeat same subject exam twice except for the subject of Engineering Mechanics. I was not lazy but somewhat careless, I didn't study on time. I passed my 1st and 3rd year in one attempt, but 2nd year was very tough for me. I wasted maximum years in passing 2nd year exam. The big hurdle was a subject Engineering Mechanics. My favourite subjects were Engineering Mathematics and Engineering Graphics. I was so adhering to Engineering Metallurgy that I corrected the mistakes of its textbook.

In my struggling days, after the Engineering, I decided to make career in the Piping Engineering. So, I studied Fluid Mechanics theory. I came across the Hardy Cross Method. After researching I came to know it's about false or lack of consideration. Yes, the educational books have their own limitations.

Because of the *"Khunnas"* of the Engineering Mechanics subject, I wrote a textbook titled "Engineering Mechanics in Easy Way", which I am publishing very soon. During my drop years, I spent most of my time in my hometown. After completing my daily studies, I would often visit my friends— Baba, Atul, Manesh, Sachin, Kiran, Tushar, Mukesh and Bittu. Spending time with them gave me a sense of relaxation and comfort, helping me unwind from the day's stress. Back then, I used to steal a few rupee coins from my mother's savings without her notice to buy cigarettes. Most of the time I used to smuggle cigarettes inside my books and sneak up to the terrace under the pretense of reading.

During my time in Loni, I experienced independence for the first time, managing responsibilities on my own. It was a phase where I learned to navigate life without constant guidance, making decisions and shaping my career path in my own unique way. I made new friends, faced academic pressures, and discovered a sense of self-reliance.

"Most of the time, I was detained due to lack of attendance for the lectures. Our college had a habit of imposing fines on students for almost every mistake, the purpose was to covey the message to parents. Once, when I got detained again, my department fined to detained students of ₹5,000 just to issue the admit card for the examination. That was a huge amount back then. The process involved filling out a challan, depositing the fine at the bank, and getting it stamped. That time, I dared to pull off a little 'challan scam.' I filled in ₹500 in the figures section and left the amount in words blank. After getting it stamped by the bank, I added another zero to the figures and wrote 'Five Thousand Only' in the words section. I submitted that modified receipt to the department and managed to get my admit card.

You can imagine how much effort went into that trick! (laughs)"

My engineering days introduced me to new friendships and a deeper connection with music, especially Bollywood songs. Over time, I built a personal collection of songs that perfectly fit every occasion and situation in life. Music became a companion that soothed my mind during difficult times. I feel grateful to have such good friends like Kiran, Tejas, Shrikant, Vishal, Sachin, Sandip, Kuldeep, Nilesh, Uday, Pramod, Vicky, Vinay, Avinash, Virendra, Kiran, Rahul, Bobby, Deepak, Vikas, Girish, Pankaj, Prashant and many more. Kiran Hegde would always sing a few lines from a song in Govinda's film *Deewana Mastana* to spread laughter:

मैंने तो हा कर दी है।

उसकी हा बाकी है।

वह जल्दिसे, हा कर दे।

थोडीसी जां बाकी है।

I have already said yes,

But I'm waiting for her yes.

I hope she says yes soon,

There's just a little life left.

Uday, Pramod, Kuldeep, Paresh, Yogesh, Bobo, Bauchar, Nilesh, Vinay, Virendra are still in touch with me and share both my good and bad times.

During the Diwali celebrations, Virendra, Vinay, Sachin, and Avinash decided to play a prank on their roommate Kiran. They carefully emptied half of a cigarette's tobacco, inserted a small roll cap cracker inside *(a roll cap cracker is a type of small firecracker or toy gun ammunition that uses a roll of paper caps containing tiny amounts of explosive material. When struck, the caps produce a small popping sound),* and then refilled the remaining half with tobacco. Kiran's roommate offered him that cigarette to smoke. Unaware of the trick, Kiran lit it and smoked normally. However, as he reached the halfway mark, the hidden cracker ignited with a sudden burst, startling him. As he reeled from the shock, his roommates burst into laughter and cheerfully wished him, **"Happy Diwali!"**

One day, I visited Virendra's room. After spending some time together, he suddenly asked, "Bandya, do you want to smoke?" I felt happy, thinking he was offering me a cigarette. I eagerly said yes, but to my surprise, he immediately replied, "Take out your own and light it!" How funny he was! I lit my own cigarette and left the room, laughing at his clever trick.

In our Suyog Bungalow, Chau always loved delivering a dialogue from a fridge advertisement. Whenever someone came near him, he would playfully act it out—first, he'd slap their back and say, **"Solid Body!"** Then, he'd tap their stomach and add, **"Good Compression!"** Finally, he'd press their bum and declare, **"Good Absorption System!"** We would all burst into laughter every time!

One of my favourite pastimes during those days was watching movies. My legs would automatically take me to the movie theatre at 9 PM. I enjoyed exploring Bollywood and Hollywood movies, even the ones with unfamiliar storylines. Whenever someone returned from watching a Hollywood movie, we had a ritual of asking about it. Our usual question was whether it was a *"theory paper"* or a *"problem-solving paper."* If the movie was heavy on dialogues and had a strong storyline, we considered it a *theory paper.* But if it was packed with action, we called it a *problem-solving paper. (Laughs)*

Some of the unforgettable movies that left a lasting impression on me include *Hum Dil De chuke Sanam*, *Munna Bhai MBBS*, *Vastav*, *Devdas*, *Veer Zara*, *Dewane*, *Who Am I?*, *My Father Is a Hero*, *Kiss of the Dragon*, *Face off*, *Black Hawk Down*, *Final Destination*, *Terminator*, *Hollow Man*, *Airforce One*, *Mr. Nice Guy*, *The Terminal*, *Vertical Limit* (In this movie, the habitual, unnecessary act of Pakistani forces bombarding India's border is depicted in one scene. The Pakistani commander says, "It's 3 AM, time to wake up Indians."). In the film *'83'*, they depict India's first Cricket World Cup victory. There is a scene where Major Sadik of Pakistan communicates via wireless to an Indian Major, assuring him that Pakistan will not carry out any bombardment on the border during the final match between India and the West Indies. This gesture ensures that they can enjoy the broadcast uninterrupted. I also liked *The Sixth Sense*, *The Fifth Element*, *Titanic*, *Die Hard*, *Tomorrow Never Dies*, *2012*, *Golden Eye*, *True Lies*, *Behind Enemy Lines*, *Poseidon*, *The Matrix*, *Mission Impossible*, *Independence Day*, *The Rock*, *Die Another Day* and many more blockbusters.

Even today, my favourite movie is *'I Am Legend'*, a story of survival and loneliness. The second one is *'Flight Plan'*, a gripping thriller that kept me on the edge of my seat with its suspenseful narrative.

Other favourites include Sairat, Mumbai Pune Mumbai, Tu Hi Re, Deool Band, Natrang, Duniyadari, Katyar Kaljat Ghusali, Aajcha Diwas Maza, Mitwa, Ek Unad Diwas, Fuss class Dabhade, Prem Mhanje Prem Mhanje Prem Aste, Hum Apke Hai Kaun, Sharabi, Anand, pk, Dangal, Guru, Hera Pheri, Hungama, Khatta Meetha, Suryawansham, Mann, Page3, Dhadkan, Dil Chata Hai, Kuch Kuch Hota Hai, Jailor (Rajnikant's), Fan, Khuda Gawah, Ghajini, A Wednesday, 3 Idiots, Naseeb (Govinda's), Apaharan, I Robot, Martian, Karate Kid. One film still on my wish list is *No Man's Land*, which famously surpassed *Lagaan* in the Oscar race—a movie I have always been curious to watch.

Due to my love for Bollywood movie songs, I own a cassette player along with a vintage collection of various movie song cassettes.

I still remember two memorable chapters from our 10th-grade Marathi textbook आपेश मरणाहून ओखटे! …..एक बखर (*Aapesh Marnahun Okhate* …a historical narrative) and अंतू बर्वा --एक व्यक्तिरेखा (*Antu Barva*….a personal character sketch) by P.L. Deshpande. These stories left a lasting impression on my mind.

A few days ago, on a weekend afternoon, I went to have tea near my hostel as usual. While there, a sentence on the wall caught my eye. It was written in a striking and attention-grabbing style, different than the usual: **"Read Ambedkar."** Seeing it sparked an instinctive desire in me to read Ambedkar's works in coming days.

Movies have always been a source of inspiration for me, leaving a lasting impact on my thoughts and expressions. One day, my engineering friend Vicky asked me how many people used to stay in your rented room. I answered, six persons. Surprisingly he asked,

"Who are they?" I answered with Nana Patekar's dialogue from *Wajood:* "*चार दीवारे, छत और मैं !*" *("Four walls, a roof, and me").* Some iconic dialogues continue to resonate in my memory even today.

A heart touching dialogue from Devdas film,

बाबूजी ने कहा गाँव छोड़ दो।

सबने कहा पारो को छोड़ दो।

पारुने कहा शराब छोड़ दो।

आज तुमने कहा हवेली छोड़ दो।

इक दिन आएगा वो कहेगा दुनियाही छोड़ दो।

(Father said, "Leave the village."
Everyone said, "Leave Paro."
Paro said, "Leave alcohol."
Today, you said, "Leave the mansion."
One day, He (God) will say, "Leave the world itself.")

One such dialogue is from the film *Khuda Gawah*:

खुदाबक्ष, इतना सोच मत।

सोच गहरी हो जाने से,

फैसले कमजोर पड जाते है।

(Khudabaksh, don't think too much.

When thoughts run too deep,

decisions become weak.)

Another memorable line is from an Ajay Devgan movie:

हमे तो अपनोंने लुटा,

गैरोमे कहा दम था।

मेरी कस्ती थी डूबी,

जहा पानी कम था।

(I was betrayed by my own;

Strangers had no strength to do so.

My boat sank

Where the water was shallow.)

I also remember so many advertising jingles. One of them I would like to share, written and casted by Javed Akhtar for a ballpoint pen advertising.

जींदगी हैं तो, ख़्वाब है।

ख़्वाब है तो, मंजिले है।

मंजिले है तो, रास्ता।

रास्ता है तो, फासला।

फासला है तो, हौसला।

के, फाइटर हमेशा जीतता है।

(If there is life, there are dreams.

If there are dreams, there are destinations.

If there are destinations, there is a path.

If there is a path, there is a distance.

If there is distance, there is courage.

Because a fighter always wins!)

I also fondly recall delivering Nana Patekar's powerful climax dialogue from '*Krantiveer*' during our hometown Ganpati festival event in the year 2000. Though I couldn't replicate Nana's distinctive accent, I memorized and performed the dialogue with great passion.

I made a wish before the Lon Tek Goddess in Loni, promising that if I passed engineering, I would offer a silver crown. However, I have yet to fulfil this promise. Nowadays, I am making provisions to fulfil it. In 2005, I pursued a degree in Mechanical Engineering from Pune University, achieving higher second class — first class in the first semester of last year, and *I am* ready to step into the professional world.

4. Early Career Struggles

After graduating in Mechanical Engineering in the 2005, I moved to Pune in search of a job, full of hope and ambition. In Pune, my school friends helped me by accommodating me in their shared room. I stayed with Arvind, Atul, Vinit, Dinesh and Piggy. I was eager to start my professional journey. To enhance my skill set, I joined a six-month classroom course on *Catia V5*, an engineering design software, in Kurve Nagar.

I commuted daily by PMT bus using a monthly pass. I studied the software diligently and practiced on its educational version to sharpen my skills. As a result, now a days, I assisted my friend Dinesh most of the time by creating 3D engineering part drawings and models for his engineering business. Dinesh has own engineering business in Pune residing with his wife Savita and two children, Dhruv and Ved.

Kalpesh, one of my friends who is no more with us. (मृत्यु जीवन का अंत नही, पूर्णता है l/ Death is not the end of life; it is completeness) He guided me the tricks of Catia V5 and provided various automobile drawings for 3D modelling practice, as he was working in a reputed automobile company.

During my engineering days, I dreamt of working in a reputed software company like *Infosys*, especially because I enjoyed creating flowcharts in my first-year engineering subject. After completing my academics, I made several attempts to master programming languages like *C++* and *C*, which would have also helped me in researching applications in *CATIA V5* software. However, despite my efforts, I couldn't grasp those languages completely.

However, reality was far more challenging than I had anticipated. I spent nearly one and a half years unemployed, facing countless rejections and struggling to find an opportunity that aligned with my qualifications. But I was happy to have made a place for myself in Pune, city of knowledge, and was planning to settle there.

One day, I went to 'Mangala,' a Movie Theatre to watch the film '*Black*'. During the interval, as the lights came on, I quickly tried to hide my face—tears had welled up in my eyes. But when I glanced to my left and right, I saw that many others in the audience were also in tears. At that moment, I let go of any hesitation and allowed my emotions to flow freely. Such was the deep emotional impact of the film *Black*, known for its powerful storytelling and intense performances. The film, directed by Sanjay Leela Bhansali, is inspired by the life of Helen Keller and revolves around a visually and hearing-impaired girl (played by Rani Mukerji) and her dedicated teacher (played by Amitabh Bachchan). Their journey of struggle, learning, and triumph is deeply moving.

Finally, in the Year 2006, after months of perseverance, I secured a job in Mumbai. I messaged Kalpesh: **"And the Buddha has Smiled,"** and he understood that I had got a job. It was a turning point—my first real step into the professional world. I relocated in Thane with the help of my friend Nilesh. I was not accustomed to the humid environment of Mumbai-*The Treasure of Sweat*. Days passed as I attended training sessions in the Shipbuilding Design department of the company. After completing the training, our team was deputed to Mazagon Dock Limited at Mumbai Dock to generate drawings and 3D models of frigates and destroyers, the war ships, using Tribon M3 software.

The company provided us with a first-class local train pass for our daily commute. On my very first day at the railway station, a local train had already arrived at the platform of Vashi station. As I hurried toward a compartment, I was shocked by the sheer crowd inside. I politely asked someone if it was a first-class coach, and he confirmed it was. With a heavy heart, I boarded, squeezing myself into the packed space. Almost instantly, I started sweating. Over time, I became accustomed to the crowd and learned to navigate my daily commute with ease.

I used to commute by bike along with my best friends—Ajinkya, Mahesh, and Abhinay when we were assigned to our Andheri office on Saturdays due to holiday at Mazagon Dock.

One evening, after office hours, Mahesh and I were riding toward Kanjurmarg station to drop him off. It was the rainy season, and as we passed in front of IIT Powai gate, my bike skidded on the muddy road, and we fell. Mahesh was thrown off, landing badly with dark mud stains on his shirt. Yet, despite the mishap, he didn't shout at me in frustration. We simply picked ourselves up and continued our journey, maintaining our daily routine as usual.

Ajinkya was a chatty person and also the team lead for our first overseas assignment in Scotland (UK). He often prepared lunch & dinner for our team using the oven provided by the hotel. On my wife's first birthday after our marriage, I hosted our first team party at overseas, where we celebrated with blended Scotch. My teammates even wished my wife a happy birthday over the phone. During that trip, I also purchased a laptop for us and a digital camera for friends and relatives as souvenirs of the experience.

One day in our Mumbai office, an intern printed his salary slip and went to the printer room to collect it. When he returned to our department, he said, "Look what I've done!" To everyone's surprise, he had accidentally printed his salary slip on an A0-sized sheet by selecting "plotter" instead of A4 in printer—a *big boom*! The entire office burst into laughter.

After starting my job at Mumbai, my parents and relatives decided it was time for me to get engaged and eventually marry. Around that time, I came across the biodata of a girl, and we arranged to meet during Diwali in 2006 at her hometown. She was the second girl I had met. In first meeting I couldn't make a firm decision about her.

After our initial meeting, her father visited us at my elder sister's house in Dhule to take the conversation forward. Following some discussions, we agreed to proceed with the marriage. I left the meeting with my cousin, Naresh Anna, feeling hopeful.

I met my fiancée in Pune for the first time after our engagement was fixed. We spent some quality time together along with my friends. During another visit, her roommates asked for a party to celebrate our match being finalized. We hosted a lunch for them in Pune, and it turned out to be a cheerful gathering. On December 31, 2006, we met again at a friend's house, and the next day, January 1, 2007, we visited the famous Lord Ganesh Temple in Chinchwad together.

Our engagement was held on February 10, 2007, in her hometown, Navapur. During the ceremony, she put a ring on my finger, and when it was my turn, I asked her, smiling, "Which finger should I wear you the ring on?" (Laughs) She pointed to the correct one, and we officially got engaged. After our engagement, we continued to meet on several occasions.

On my request my fiancée used to give me a wakeup call every day at sharp 6'O clock in the morning, so I could reach to the local station on time.

5. Marriage and Stability in Mumbai

Eventually, I accepted that software programming wasn't my path. Instead, I wished to marry a girl who would be a computer engineer — someone who could fulfil the dream that I couldn't achieve. Destiny played its part, and I married a computer engineer, Yogini, on 21st April 2007 and began my married life in Airoli, Navi Mumbai, where we rented a house.

घर हे दोघांच असतं, ते दोघांनी सावरायचं असतं.

एकाने पसरवलं तर, दुसऱ्याने आवरायचे असतं.

(A home belongs to both, and both must take care of it.

If one spreads the mess, the other should tidy it up.)

Due to my overseas trip to Scotland, the very next day of our wedding, we couldn't celebrate our honeymoon. Scotland is a country that's part of the United Kingdom, known for its stunning landscapes, rich history, and unique culture, including bagpipes, whisky, and the Loch Ness monster. After returning from overseas work, I took a long leave. But my manager called me back midway, shortening my leave due to urgent work at the office. I immediately reported to duty. So, we planned our honeymoon for the following year and flew to Goa to celebrate.

On the very first day after I returned from overseas, Yogini complained about my mother's behaviour toward her. She told me that while I was away, she was alone in Erandol, and my mother imposed many restrictions on her. I was very loyal to my wife, loved her very much, and she also balanced the family routine in an excellent way. Life seemed to be on track. Yogini was a wonderful cook. We were both non-vegetarian—she preferred chicken, while I favoured mutton. She disliked curd, while I liked it most. She had practiced to cook my favourite dish after discussing it with my mother. Every day, she packed my tiffin with food I liked, but at times, she would lovingly insist that I eat vegetables I wasn't fond of, like bitter gourd. She had a special way of preparing it to remove its bitterness. On every festival, she would cook a traditional feast, making the occasion even more special. I never watched a single movie in a cinema hall without her. Most weekends, I planned outings to watch new releases. Her favourite song was 'Kehne ko jashna bahara hai' from the Jodha Akbar movie. One day, she suggested we watch the film '*No Smoking,*' with John Abraham in the lead role. I was laughing while watching the movie because the movie was not serving the purpose for what she planned. The movie was so boring. Many times, I asked her to leave the cinema hall, but she insisted on staying until the end. Most of the time, she refused me permission to have a smoke. Apart from office parties, I never consumed alcohol without her presence. Whenever we went out for dinner, she would set a predefined limit for me, and I always adhered to it. No matter how much I drank, I never fought with her after consuming alcohol. We often visited our friends, and colleagues' families on weekends.

One day, she jokingly commented on the shirt I wore during our first meeting, saying she didn't like the colour. I teased her, asking, "Then why did you say yes to me?" She just shook her head with a smile, and I didn't ask her the reason of saying yes to me

On another day, she asked, "Can you sing?" I replied, "Yes," and she urged me to sing for her. I was used to singing and performed with great passion, choosing heartfelt songs that truly touched the moment.

Yogini always kept the house neat and clean. One day, my wife asked me if we could visit her parental home in Navapur for ten days. Surprised, I responded by sharing a story from P.L. Deshpande, the legendary Marathi author known for his vast literary contributions.

In one of his writings, he described a son-in-law visiting his wife's parental home. For the first two or three days, his father-in-law treated him with great hospitality. However, as the days passed, the son-in-law extended his stay beyond what his father-in-law had expected. Eventually, the father-in-law, running out of patience, assigned him the task of levelling the courtyard— (the act of levelling or smoothing a courtyard, often done using cow dung in rural areas). I then told my wife the moral of the story: *"Just because the sugarcane is sweet, you shouldn't eat it roots and all."* (Meaning: Enjoy something in moderation; don't overindulge or take undue advantage.)

When I met Yogini for the first time in Pune, I gifted her a teddy bear. One day after our marriage, she asked me, "The first gift you gave me—the teddy—wasn't your choice, was it? Smita (Arvind's wife) bought it from a shop." I admitted it was true but explained the situation. I had travelled from Mumbai to Pune by bus and reached my friend's home, where all my friends had gathered to meet me. Smita and Arvind were about to leave urgently on their bike, and I had no time to go shopping myself. Since Yogini was calling me repeatedly, I didn't want to keep her waiting. So, I asked Smita to pick out a beautiful gift for Yogini, and she did. Yogini, however, placed that teddy in a cupboard and never looked at it again. To this day, she brings up this incident whenever we have a debate. At that time, I was about to get married for the first time, and I was still learning to understand her feelings.

      Unfortunately, my wife couldn't secure any job opportunity after our marriage. After three years of married life, she decided to focus on starting a family. On 8th April 2010, we were blessed with a baby boy, a precious gift, 'Jivitesh,' in our lives.

      During Jivitesh's first Diwali, when he was about six months old, we all gathered in my hometown, Erandol, to celebrate. My little nephews and nieces also joined us, filling the house with joy. That night, we lit fireworks for a long time, enjoying the festive spirit. At the same time, Tushar's grandmother approached Yogini and asked how she was protecting Jivitesh from the loud cracker sounds, as the kids were enthusiastically bursting them. Yogini calmly replied that she had placed small pieces of cotton in Jivitesh's ears. She was deeply caring toward him while also ensuring that the children could enjoy the celebrations without restrictions. When Jivitesh grew up, Yogini decided to buy cow's milk for him instead of the regular buffalo milk. However, I was accustomed to buffalo milk and resisted the change. She shouted at me, asking if I couldn't make a small adjustment for our child. I began to feel that her care and attention were shifting more towards Jivitesh than me. With no other choice, I reluctantly started adjusting by drinking tea without cream. Sometimes, Yogini would shout at Jivitesh for his mischievous behaviour. In response, he would suddenly run to me, seeking my support. However, he didn't realize that I couldn't protect him—nor could anyone else. Ironically, I am still searching support for myself against her. *(Laughs)*

Once, I bought a small boxing kit for 'J' **(I used to call Jivitesh as 'J')**. Whenever he demanded for something, I used to tell him to punch the boxing bag hard by saying, *"Got a Punch,"* and he always did. One day, I playfully told J to hit me with the boxing gloves. He struck me so hard—twice—that, in an instant, his mother took away his gloves and J came towards me again. off course we both were helpless and could not do anything about it.

On my first visit to Yogini's maternal home, she invited me to play chess with her. I started with great confidence, but within five minutes, she checkmated me, sharing a laugh with her father. I felt quite nervous at that moment. Later, in Mumbai, we played eleven chess games, and I won every single one. Eventually, she gave up and decided never to play with me again. *(Laughs)*

Most of the time, Yogini argues with me for not taking her along during my overseas assignments. The first time my parents visited our home in Airoli, I called my father after leaving the office and asked him to bring some milk from the grocery store. That night, Yogini questioned me, *"Why did you call your father instead of asking me?"* She was so unreasonable that she started arguing loudly in front of my parents. The very next day, my parents left Airoli, saying goodbye and giving us their blessings. Actually, Yogini failed to build a good relationship with my mother and elder sister, or vice versa. Yogini had good tuning with my younger sister,

Sunita. Since my mother and sisters did not attend the naming ceremony of my son, J.

On another occasion, my cousin Chotu Dada visited us and brought wheat grains from his fields as a gesture of goodwill. However, Yogini refused to accept them. Another one time, my cousin Dilip Nana called from Mumbai Airport, expressing his wish to meet us with his family and a friend. I guided him on how to reach Airoli and ended the call. Immediately, Yogini told me to call him back and ask him not to come, saying, *"I'm pregnant, and I won't be able to serve them."* I refused, explaining that he was my brother and I couldn't turn him away. I assured her that they would manage on their own and wouldn't be a burden. But she wouldn't listen. With a heavy heart, I called him back and told him that Yogini wasn't feeling well, so it would be best to change his plans. He understood and cancelled his visit.

To this day, I feel ashamed of Yogini's behaviour and stubbornness in such moments.

I worked hard and stayed committed to my job, spending six years in the same organization in Mumbai. I was happy with *Dal-Chawal,* but Yogini had some more expectations. However, over time, I began to feel stagnant. The passion and enthusiasm I once had started to fade. My job became routine, and I found myself merely existing in the workplace without true engagement.

In the Year 2010, I was introduced to the smartphone for the first time. Yogini, excitedly, pointed out that smart technology had arrived in the market. In response, I made a casual observation—perhaps more of a guess—that the technology now made available to the public might have already been in use by military forces or the agencies. This assumption was entirely based on my intuition, without any confirmation, but it reflected how my thoughts often leaned toward the future while I was still living in the present. I wanted to fulfil my wish of owning a season cricket ball, but my wife refused to let me buy it.

      In the month of March of the Year 2012, an unexpected event changed everything. My boss asked me to resign. I asked the reason, but he did not explain. For more than a year I was a single person serving my department by working on Catia V5. Since the organisation was tied up with different software developer company rather than Dassault System. Without hesitation, I signed the resignation letter, unaware of the struggles that lay ahead. A few days later, I found out that I wasn't alone—around 200 other employees had also been laid off because of lack of new project work. Before few months of leaving my job, I brought my new home at Airoli. Also, I started experiencing an unsettling fear, as if someone was chasing me from my office to my home. My heart would race, and my mind was consumed with anxiety. I had discussed this anxiety with my superiors too before receiving the layoff.

6. Uncertainty and Financial Struggles

At the time, my wife and I were living with our two-year-old son in the home we had purchased in November 2011. Losing my job was a devastating blow. I had no idea what the future held. I searched tirelessly for a new job, relying on my experience, but the market was tough. After facing repeated disappointments, I decided to explore freelancing. However, after two successful projects, I was left jobless again.

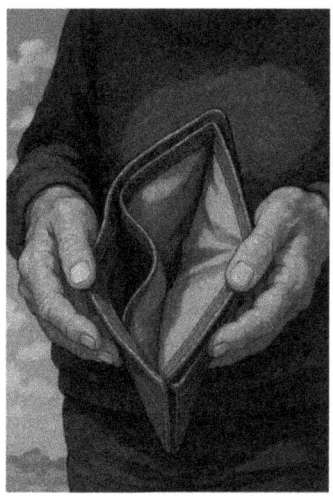

In desperation, I took a job in a passenger vehicle service to earn whatever I could. The salary was meagre, barely enough to support my family. After three months, I managed to find a contract job in my engineering field for one year. It was temporary, but my family was relieved, hoping that better days were ahead. However, life had other plans. When the contract ended, I found myself unemployed again. Still, I did not convey this to my wife, believing I could secure a new job within a few days. Every morning, I visited a cybercafé to apply for jobs, and in the afternoons, I would spend time at a park or a bus stop. I reached out to several friends, requesting their help in finding a job. After a month of persistent efforts, I finally shared my situation with my wife. Financial strain began to mount—home loan EMIs, school fees, and daily expenses became overwhelming. My wife's trust in me started to fade, and tension grew in our relationship.

I applied relentlessly for jobs but faced repeated rejections. One day, I thought of visiting Shri Balaji Temple at Tirumala to seek divine blessings. However, due to insufficient funds, I couldn't afford the journey. Instead, I visited the local Balaji Temple in Airoli and offered my prayers with devotion. As a mark of surrender and faith, I shaved my head at a nearby salon.

Finally, after much effort, I landed a job overseas in Qatar in the year 2016. Qatar is a peninsular Arab country whose terrain comprises arid desert and a long Persian (Arab) Gulf shoreline of beaches and dunes. Also on the coast is the capital, Doha, known for its futuristic skyscrapers and other ultramodern architecture inspired by ancient Islamic design, such as the limestone Museum of Islamic Art. Though the salary was lower than expected, I saw it as an opportunity. It was my second overseas job, the first being in 2007. But once again, my employer forced me to resign without explaining the reason, and I had no choice but to return home. I told my wife that the project had ended, but she did not believe me.

From that moment, our relationship deteriorated. She became distant, often misbehaving with me. I endured it for the sake of our son. As time passed, my situation worsened. She refused to listen or support me. In those days, my wife neither allowed me to eat the food prepared by her nor offered me a single cup of tea. She often reminded me that the groceries at home were provided by her parents and insisted that I find a job and earn my own money. One afternoon at lunchtime, for reasons unknown, she handed me a mango. Overwhelmed by hunger, I ate the mango along with its peel and drank water to satisfy my hunger.

During my unemployment, Yogini often reminded me that love and affection alone could not sustain a family. Whenever I reassured her that I would soon secure a job, trying to console her with warmth and affection, she would respond with the stark reality that the world runs on money. "The grocery man—the 'Baniya'—will never ask for love and affection but will demand payment before delivering goods," she would say. Her words, though harsh, were rooted in truth, emphasizing the importance of financial stability and family responsibility.

One day, for a mood change, I went to watch the movie *Sairat* alone, as Yogini had remained silent with me. After returning home, Yogini passed a comment, "See Jivitesh, he went to the movie *Sairat* alone." Still, I am thinking, how would she have known where I had been that day?

However, her constant taunts and verbal attacks often pushed me to the edge. Her arrogance and relentless criticism would ignite my temper, leading to heated arguments. In moments of uncontrollable anger, I crossed lines I deeply regret. I used abusive language, cursed her, and, on two or three occasions, raised my hand against her, breaking her glasses in the heat of the moment. Each time, she would break down in tears and call her parents.

One day, her parents came to Airoli to confront me. They spoke harshly, pointing fingers at me with anger and disdain. The tension escalated, and in a fit of rage, I lost control, striking them with my hands and bare feet. They were three and I was alone. The very next day, Yogini filed a case of domestic violence against me.

Feeling broken and ashamed, I left Airoli and returned home, carrying the weight of my actions and the consequences that followed. I never missed a court date, regularly traveling from Erandol to CBD Belapur to attend the hearings. During this difficult time, Nitin Bhau, a police inspector from Thane, kindly helped me in arranging day accommodations in CBD Belapur while the case was ongoing.

In February 2019, I secured a job in Bhiwandi, working on the installation of Industrial Water Purification Systems. I was deputed onsite for installation purposes, but I took the job solely out of necessity, as I was unemployed at the time. During those days, Yogini presented me with an offer: if I agreed to gift deed our home to her, she would withdraw the domestic violence case against me. I agreed and went to the registrar's office in Kalwa to complete the process. By a stroke of luck, I ran into J there after a long time. J made himself busy in playing with my smart phone. Yogini was accompanied by her lawyer for the formalities. I signed the gift deed and, after a brief conversation, said goodbye to J and left for Bhiwandi. At the next hearing, Yogini formally withdrew the case. The lady judge instructed her to write 'unconditional withdrawal' as the reason on the application form and firmly warned her not to approach the court again for a similar matter.

After eight months, the physical strain and stress started affecting my health, so I discussed quitting with my father. However, he strongly opposed my decision and warned me, "If you resign from this job, don't come home."

Despite his words, I struggled to continue for another month before finally deciding to resign. When I returned to my hometown, the moment I stepped into the house, my father confronted me, asking, "Why did you leave the job? Have you come here to eat free bread?"

I silently put down my luggage and walked away. This was the first job I left by my own choice. Though my parents continued to provide me food without hesitation, I could sense their uneasiness.

Shortly after, the COVID-19 pandemic struck, shattering any hope of finding a new job. I kept myself occupied by working on my laptop, trying to stay productive despite the uncertainty.

Then, in the Year 2020, life took a turn—I got a job at Lemma, and my journey restarted once again.

7. A Life-Altering Experience (Year 2016 – The Turning Point)

Then, in the Year 2016, something inexplicable happened—an experience that changed my life forever.

One ordinary day, while watching television alone, I suddenly heard a familiar voice. It was the voice of a friend, but strangely, it was not coming from the television. Confused, I focused more intently. Then, the voice spoke again—this time, it addressed me directly.

Shocked, I instinctively turned toward the **window**, trying to locate the source. But the voice responded, as if aware of my thoughts: **"Why are you looking at the window?"**

Panic gripped me. I knew no one was there, yet the voice continued. **"Change the television channel."**

That meant they could visualise what I was seeing.

Terror surged through me. This voice was not external—it was speaking directly inside my mind. I was shocked and could not recognise where the sound was coming from. I was afraid because that sound was directly hitting my eardrum. I was hearing that sound wirelessly, without any device.

As I reflected on my past, I realized that these experiences had not started in 2016. The first unnoticed signs had appeared much earlier, around 2012. I had moments of irrational fear, difficulty concentrating, and an overwhelming sense of being controlled. At the time, I had brushed them aside, attributing them to stress and exhaustion. But now, everything felt disturbingly real.

Over time, the sensation intensified. I became convinced that my mind had been hacked, much like a computer. It felt as though my thoughts and actions were being manipulated by an external force—an invisible presence that had invaded my consciousness. My mobile phone and computer system were also hacked. When I shared this with my wife, she replied, "Are you any tycoon for someone to hack your systems?" She did not agree with me.

I struggled to make sense of what was happening to me. Was it reality? Was I losing control over my own mind?

I confided in my wife, parents, and friends. They advised me to seek medical help. Though I was reluctant, I had no choice. But during this time, I started writing about the things I experienced. I also continued searching for jobs, as I had a family to support. However, my struggle only deepened. Desperate for work, I even visited the district collector's office to seek employment opportunities. The collector was so cool and seemed responsible. He very humbly asked me, "Did you not try for your job?"

I said, "I tried a lot and have come to you for my last hope."

He said, "All right," and kept my application in his records. Though the collector listened to me kindly, no immediate help came. The days were passing in difficult situations.

My life became unbearable. I suffered from terrifying nightmares and woke up feeling as though I was being controlled. It was as if my body was not mine, as if I was merely a **puppet**. I constantly questioned myself: **"When was I truly me?"** It felt like my consciousness was being overridden by an unknown entity.

My condition worsened. Even in crowded places, I heard voices warning me, "Do not ask that."(नको वीचारु ते!) It was as if everyone around me—strangers, passersby—were warning me not to question what was happening. The world that once made sense had collapsed, replaced by an unexplainable nightmare. I came to a firm decision that some external power or force or unknown entity was handling my thoughts, my movements, my entire life. I felt myself being **hypnotised** with horror dreams. My body felt controlled by some external power, giving a feeling of a "False Body." So, I had a feeling of, **"When I was Me?"** because the moment I had lived was not mine, it was lived by somebody who was within me or controlling me.

I visited a doctor, **a neuropsychiatrist,** at my family's insistence. I had no answers of my own, and I was desperate to understand what was happening to me. Sitting in the doctor's office, I explained everything—the voices, the loss of control, the feeling of being hacked, and the terrifying realization that I could no longer tell when I was truly myself. After listening carefully to my experiences, then, after a moment of silence, he looked at me and said, **"You are suffering from schizophrenia."**

The doctor diagnosed me with schizophrenia. He explained that it was caused by chemical imbalances in the brain and he prescribed medication. He encouraged me, saying that things would improve. His words felt distant, almost unreal. Schizophrenia? I had never considered such a possibility. For the next several months, I took the pills regularly. Slowly, I began to notice some changes. The voices were reduced, the nightmares were not as frequent, and my mind felt a little more at peace.

You can't imagine the trouble I was in. My nights turned into horrific nightmares, and I often woke up in a state of pure terror. It felt as though I was being hypnotized, as if someone had taken complete control of my body. It was no longer mine—I was merely an observer, trapped inside a false body. I reached a terrifying realization: an external force was handling my thoughts, my movements, my entire life. I was no longer in control. Due to the effects of my medication, I often felt drowsy, but Yogini wouldn't let me rest. She would shout at me, saying, "Don't sleep inside the house! Go outside and find a job." One day, feeling overwhelmed, I called my father and asked him to request my medicine be replaced with a lower dose.

When Was I Truly "Me"?

This question haunted me: "When was I really me?"

The moments I lived no longer felt like my own. Someone—or something—was within me, dictating my actions, my thoughts, my very existence. It was as if my identity had been hijacked.

I felt like I had been abandoned in a vast, endless desert—without water, without hope. I always challenge them to open themselves or kill me. I searched for answers, but there were none. Desperation turned to rage, and in my mind, I cursed the unseen forces that tormented me. But my defiance was useless—I was met only with silence and helplessness.

As I was losing my savings for our daily expenses. I start borrowing money from my friends and relatives. My friend Arvind helps me most in those critical situations. As Yogini has raised domestic violence petition against me, I appeared on every date by travelling my home town. In 2019 she withdrawal case on one condition that I should gift our Airoli home to her and I did it. Since, from 2016 as I was away from my family. I did not pay a single penny to her till date.

In the Year 2019, while working in Bhiwandi, she invited me to stay with J at our home in Airoli for the gift deed process. After signing the documents, we lived together as a seemingly happy family. However, just three or four days later, things took a turn—she stopped cooking for me and began demanding money for J's school fees. She also withdrew from any communication, refusing to speak with me.

Feeling isolated and overwhelmed, I became distressed and, in a moment of despair, bought a rope with the intention of ending my life. I wrote a suicide note and placed it in my luggage. Though I attempted to follow through multiple times, I couldn't summon the courage to go through with it.

A few days later, one evening, while I was alone at home, the doorbell rang. When I opened the door, I found a policeman standing outside. He asked for my name and instructed me to accompany him to the Rabale police station. Confused, I asked why I was being taken there. He replied that your wife had reported your suicide note.

At the police station, I saw Yogini, J, and her lawyer waiting. The officers questioned me and then turned to Yogini, asking if she wanted to file a complaint. She agreed, and they registered a complaint, stating that J had discovered the rope and the suicide note in my luggage. After completing the formalities, the police allowed me to leave.

When I returned home around 3 AM, I found my luggage placed outside the door. I knocked, and after some time, Yogini opened the door, ordering me to leave immediately. I pleaded with her, but our conversation escalated into an argument. She called her lawyer and created a scene. Eventually, she told me that she would allow me inside only if I left early in the morning with my belongings. In frustration, I showed her my middle finger, and as expected, she slammed the door shut.

With nowhere else to go, I carried my luggage to the apartment's staircase landing, and spent the night there. At dawn, I gathered myself and left for work, carrying my bags along with me.

8. Was It Really Just a Fantasy?

At a same time, I was visiting a doctor, a lawyer and the police station. After a few months, I visited the doctor again. He smiled and asked:

"So, all that you had experienced was a fantasy, right?"

But I knew the answer in my heart. I shook my head and replied:

"No, that was not a fantasy. It was real—because I had experienced it."

The doctor looked at me, perhaps expecting a different response. But how could I deny something I had lived through? The voices, the loss of control, the feeling of being trapped inside a **false body**—these were not just illusions. They were as real as the ground beneath my feet.

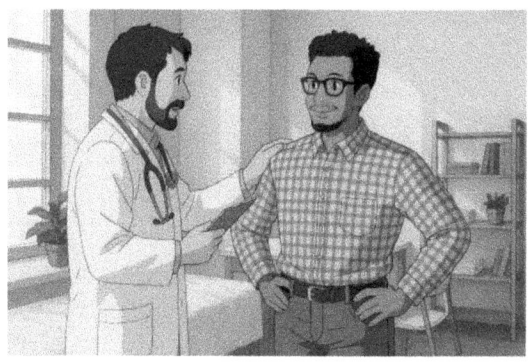

I confirmed with the doctor whether I had been admitted to the hospital, as I did not remember at that time. He replied to me that I was admitted to his hospital for 10 days.

I asked my doctor a question: can I share all this with someone in my office? He replied, "No." He also refused me permission to share it with my wife either. He told me neither one would support you nor understand. He wrote the next prescription, and I purchased the medicine.

After prescribing multiple medications, he also advised me to exercise regularly. At every visit, he checks and confirms my oxygen level and blood pressure. He recommends a morning diet of dates and almonds and suggests avoiding seafood. Honestly, I neither exercise regularly nor completely refrain from eating seafood, indulging in it once every two months. After a few years, I requested him to stop the medication, as I felt I no longer needed it. He firmly responded, "Who is the doctor here? Who will decide when to stop the medicine?" Out of great respect for him, I continued taking the prescribed medication diligently.

Let me make one thing clear—my life is not a fantasy. This book's content is non-fiction, based on true incidents, my experiences, and my beliefs.

9. The Struggle for Control

Most days passed without trouble, but the biggest question remained unanswered:

"If I was hacked, then when was I truly myself?"

If I was hacked and I can't decide when I was with my own soul and **When I was truly 'Me'.**

Even as I continued taking the prescribed medication, I still heard voices in unexpected places—even inside an airplane. I pleaded with them, begged them to stop. But nothing worked.

I asked them directly: **"Who are you?"**

Sometimes, they replied, **"We are God."**

Other times, they said, **"We are in jail."**

Sometimes the voice said the **dead** were speaking to me.

Most of the time, the things that I handled would fall out suddenly, and at that time, the voice said, "Look, the accidents happen in such a way."

You can observe theatre artists in their play delivering the dialogues like a recorded cassette. Of course, practice makes man perfect, and the artist practices, but I am sure that things happen in another way.

Their responses only deepened my confusion. Who were they? What did they want from me?

During my jobless days, when I had spare time at home, I dedicated every moment to my son **'J'**. I poured into him everything that I had learned before he came into this world — storytelling, playing different games, and singing songs just for him. Every night, he became habitual of listening to my stories, and I gave him all the knowledge I was aware of.

Trust me! if you have practised in writing essays in school, it helps in storytelling. I used to sing lullabies for him too. I even tried telling the stories of his favourite cartoons — Timmy from "Shaun the Sheep," and Bheem from "Chhota Bheem". I used to tell him the story about 'Bheem-Bakasur' battle in the Mahabharat too.

I developed the habit of using "J" to memorize our home address while playing the 'Thief & Police' game.

As days passed, he started growing, and our bond grew stronger. We often played cricket in the hall — I always bowled, and while bowling, I counted the balls aloud: **1-2-3-4-5**. When it came to **five**, I would intentionally pronounce it as **"FIVE"**, and every time he would correct me with his innocent voice, saying, **"Pappa, not FIVE — it's PHI."** I always smiled, thinking of asking him one day, when he grows up, **how would you read 5 Φ?**

During his nursery school days, I always went to drop him off. As soon as he saw the school, he would start crying. I used to drop him off like a jailor escorting a prisoner and would cry myself after leaving him. Well, I was no different — all parents do the same.

When we went on outings with his bicycle, he was 10 years old — such a mischievous boy. He would pedal fast and shout, "Pappa, run!" 'कमीना' मुझे दौड़ाता था। समझमे नहीं आता था की मैं उसे घुमाने लाया हू की वो मुझे?

That rascal used to make me run. I couldn't understand whether I had brought him out for a walk or he had brought me.

I have been away from him since 2016; I met J for five minutes in 2022. Now he has grown up and is 15 years old. These days, he sends me cold and unfriendly voice messages — influenced by his mother. He has forgotten a father's love and can't seem to recall the affection I once showered upon him. My situation feels like Kamal Hasan's character in the movie *Sadma*, especially in the heartbreaking last train scene.

Time changes everything, but a father's heart remains the same — always full of love.

Those days were not only for him — I also spent time nurturing myself. I indulged in reading books on my favourite subjects: English and Marathi Grammar. While studying English grammar, I discovered a fascinating rule — that every word starting with the letter 'Q' is always followed by the letter 'U'. This sparked an idea in my mind — to design T-shirts with the letter 'Q' for males and 'U' for females, symbolizing that **QU** is the perfect combination for a perfect couple.

For your knowledge, the word **'Queue'** is grammatically correct, but **'Qatar'** defies this rule of 'QU'.

In Marathi literature, I cherished my memories by revisiting the beauty of grammar with the Alankar ("figure of speech" or "ornamentation"). I used to read the school textbooks of Marathi belonging to my relatives. Here are a few examples that I hold close to my heart:

स्वभावोक्ति अलंकार :

मातीत ते पसरले अतिरम्य पंख.

केले वरी उदर पांडुर निष्कलंक.

चंचू तशीच उघडी आणि पदही लाम्बविले.

निष्प्राण देह पड़ला, श्रमही निमाले.

Swabhavokti Alankar: "Swabhavokti Figure of Speech" or "Natural Description".

The soil was spread with the enchanting wings,

Its belly turned upward — pure, spotless, white,

The beak lay open, and the legs stretched out,

The lifeless body fell — its weariness finally rested.

अतिशोयक्ति अलंकार :

गणपत वाणी विडी पितांना चावायाचा नुसतीच काडी.

अण् म्हणायचा मनाशिचकी ह्या जागेवर बांधिन माड़ी.

आणि मिचकाउनी मग उजवा डोळा आणि उड़वूनी डावी भिवई,

भिरकाउनी तो तशीच द्यायचा लकेर बेचव जैसी गवई.

Atishyokti Alankar: "Hyperbole"

Ganpat Vani would only chew the bidi stick,

And silently think — *On this very spot, I'll build a mansion!*

With a playful wink of his right eye, and flicking his left eyebrow,

He would toss out the tasteless smoke, just like a village singer dismisses an off-tune note.

अनुप्रास अलंकार:

काकूने काकाच्या कोटातील कामाची कागदे

कात्रिने कराकरा कापून काढले.

Anupras Alankar: "Alliteration".

Aunt cut the important papers from uncle's coat,

With scissors, making a sharp *karakara* sound.

दृष्टांत अलंकारः

लहानपण देगा देवा,

मुंगी साखरेचा रवा.

ऐरावत रत्न थोर,

त्यासी अंकुशाचा मार.

Drushtant Alankar: "Example-based Simile" or simply "Analogy".

O God! give back my childhood,

Like an ant with a heap of sugar grains,

The mighty elephant, adorned with precious gems,

Yet controlled by a small goad's strike.

    These small things gave me peace and made me feel alive even during the darkest days. They reminded me that knowledge is never wasted, and time spent with loved ones is the greatest treasure one can ever have.

    I believe life is not always about chasing after big dreams but cherishing the small blessings around us. Those simple yet precious moments with my son became the foundation of my strength. Even though I was jobless and surrounded by uncertainty, I realized that happiness lies in what we give, not what we receive.

    If there is one message I want to share with the world, it is this — Acceptance and Moving Forward. Life may leave many questions unanswered, but the secret is to focus on what lies ahead rather than on what is left behind.

This book is not just my story — it is my voice, hoping to reach someone out there who needs the same support I once longed for. If even one soul finds strength through my journey, then every struggle I endured would have found its true purpose.

Besides that, I developed a habit of identifying car companies and their models by recognizing their styling and exterior trims. It brings me immense joy when my guesses turn out to be correct. I have a particular preference for sedans over SUVs and Hatchbacks and I am especially in love with blue BMW sedans because of its beautifully designed nose.

My aesthetic sense helps me pair the perfect colour with a specific car model. For example, BMW, Mahindra's XUV700 and Maruti Suzuki's Baleno shine best in blue, Swift in red with black roof, Mercedes-Benz and Audi in white, Volkswagen's Polo stands out in red, and Toyota's Fortuner looks most striking in white, Skoda's and Honda's are best in grey shades, Kia Carnival in black.

I have a habit of noticing the slogans (quotations) written on the back of trucks by their owners. These slogans reflect their creativity, and I have a special collection of them. Here are some of my favourites:

रेहमत तेरी, मेहनत मेरी।

(Your blessings, my hard work)

मालिक की गाड़ी, ड्राइवर का पसीना।

चलती है रोड पर, बनके हसीना।

(Owner's truck, driver's sweat,
Runs on the road, like a beauty set.)

पाहतोस काय रागाने? ओवरटेक केला वाघाने.

(Why stare at me with anger?
You've been overtaken by a tiger!)

पहिले थे दीवाने,अब लगे है कमाने।

(Once we were crazy in love, now we're busy in earning)

Prepare for the worst!

Hope for the best!

मैंने दिल से कहा, ढूंढ लाना खुशी।

नासमझ गम ले आया, गम ही सही।

(I told my heart, "Go find happiness."
The naive heart brought sorrow instead—well, sorrow it is.)

गुण तो ना था कोई, अवगुण मेरे भुला देना।

(I had no virtues, but please forget my flaws.)

मेरी नजर में वह चढ़ गया, रुतबे में और बढ़ गया।

(He rose in my eyes, and his stature grew even more)

प्यार तो होना ही था।

(Love was bound to happen.)

जमीन पे ना सही, आसमां में आ मील।

तेरे बिना गुजारा, ए दिल है मुश्किल।

(If not on the ground, meet me in the sky.
Living without you is difficult, oh heart.)

जूनून हैं मेरा, बनू मैं तेरे काबिल।

(It is my passion to become worthy of you.)

तेरी राहों से, तेरी बाहों से यू ना जाऊंगा मैं।

ये इरादा हैं, मेरा वादा हैं लौट आऊंगा मैं।

(I won't walk away from your path or your embrace.
It's my resolve, it's my promise—I will return.)

हद से गुजरना नहीं इश्कमें, जो मिला है नसीब से।

(Don't go beyond limits in love; what you receive is destined)

मी थेट शेतात चालली आहे.

(I am going straight to the farm.)

मन का हुआ तो अच्छा, नहीं हुआ तो और भी अच्छा।
(If things go my way, it's good; if not, it's even better.)

इक अर्सा हुआ मुस्कराये हुए।
(It's been ages since I last smiled.)

हम बोलेगा तो बोलेंगे की बोलता है।
(If I speak, they'll say, "Look, he's speaking!")

Future belongs to those, who dare.

ये सितारे गिननेवालो, इक और चांदनी आ गयी,
जरा फिरसे गिनती कर लो।
(Oh, you who count the stars,
A new moonlight has arrived—
Go on, count once more.)

तू वर्गात मी स्वर्गात.
(You are in the classroom, and I am in heaven.)

ऐसा ही हू मैं।
(That's just the way I am.)

During my arduous struggle, I remained completely away from smoking and alcohol for nearly three years — two years during my toughest days and one year amidst the COVID pandemic.

Do you know what I did in the summer of Covid-19 pandemic? I channelled my time and efforts into productive endeavours. I rewrote my engineering seminar on "Adaptive Headlamp System", refining it into a more innovative concept. Additionally, I compiled a comprehensive collection of engineering formulas and fundamental principles into a structured document.

My studies extended into fire-fighting sprinkler systems, where I delved deep into their design. I developed a specialized fire protection project for a bakery area, during which I formulated a unique equation for the K-factor—a crucial parameter in water sprinkler systems. This formula is not documented in any existing books.

Furthermore, I authored and published a white paper titled 'Project Crashing Using Critical Path Method' on *Project management.com*, on project management in fire safety, specifically tailored for bakery areas. I also began writing a book titled "Engineering Mechanics in Easy Way", aimed at simplifying complex engineering concepts.

Amidst my technical work, I continued my habit of noticing and collecting slogans and witty quotations inscribed on the backs of trucks, admiring the creativity of their owners.

10. A Life Like a Movie

It felt like my situation had been cast as the lead actor in a surreal Marathi movie—just like the protagonist in **'Aga Bai Arechhya'**, who experiences an uncontrollable phenomenon.

Similarly, another fundamental is used in Tom Cruise's Hollywood movie **'Minority Report'.** Set in the year **2054**, the film explores a future where a specialized police department called **Precrime** apprehends criminals based on **foreknowledge** provided by three psychics known as **Precogs**. These psychics can foresee crimes before they happen, allowing law enforcement to stop them in advance.

Tom Cruise plays John Anderton, a Precrime officer who becomes a fugitive when the system predicts that *he* will commit a murder in the near future. The film follows his quest to prove his innocence and uncover flaws in the system.

Themes:

- Free will vs. determinism.
- Surveillance and privacy.
- The morality of punishing crimes before they're committed.
- **Memory reading** (or accessing visions from the Precogs' minds) is a key concept in Minority Report—but it's not memory in the traditional sense. Instead, the film features precognitive visions of the future, which are recorded and reviewed by the Precrime unit.

- However, some aspects feel similar to memory reading:

In the Hollywood movie **'Independence Day'**, an alien uses a human body to communicate with the officials.

Or perhaps, my life had become something even more extraordinary—like the Hollywood movie **'Avatar'**, where a person exists inside a different body, controlled by an external force.

I also watched the movie **'Ra-One,'** starring Shahrukh Khan. The movie's concept left me with an unsettling feeling—almost as if it resonated with my belief that someone might be using me as a **'guinea pig'** for experimental purposes. This suspicion lingered in my mind, adding another layer of complexity to my understanding of my own life and experiences.

One day, Yogini and I were watching a show, *India's Got Talent*. In that episode, a magician was demonstrating his skill of black magic. He held a doll in his hand and made the host comfortable in a chair. Moments later, the magician pierced a needle into the doll, and the host visibly flinched, feeling pain at the exact instant. Trust me, guys, I felt like I was the victim of that broadcast. I was completely shocked, but my wife showed no visible expressions, as if nothing unusual had happened.

Was I truly living my own life? Or was I just a spectator, watching myself from the outside?

My marriage suffered immensely due to I did not have sufficient money. My wife refused to believe my experiences and often called me insane. With no job, no money, and increasing debts, I was drowning in despair. I had borrowed large sums from friends and relatives, but financial help was only a temporary solution. My wife's behaviour worsened—she verbally abused me multiple times a day.

In those days, I remembered that girl in 8th standard and came to some 4 lines written by Mr. Chandrashekhar B. Gokhale,

आपण आवडावे त्याला,

ज्याला आपण आवडतो.

नाहीतर आपल्या आवडीसाठी,

आपण उगाच आयुष्य दवडतो.

You should like the one,

Who truly likes you.

Otherwise, for your own liking,

You simply waste your life.

Somebody expects from our true love,

तू जवळ असली की,

मला माझाही आधार लागत नाही.

तू फक्त सोबत रहा,
मी दूसरे काहीही मागत नाही.

When you are near,
I don't even need my own support.
Just stay by my side,
I ask for nothing more.

Now, the life picture explains,
जळण्यासाठी तोडलेल्या ओंडक्याला,
एकदा पालवी फुटली.
त्यालाच कळेना,
ही जगायची जीद्द कुठली?

A log cut down to burn,
Once sprouted fresh leaves in return.
It wondered in surprise,
From where did this will to live arise.

With deep admiration for Gulzar Sahab, I dared to rewrite the *Lakdi Ki Kathi* song's three new Antara for my son J. I would often sing the song repeatedly, ensuring that J memorized it too. These small moments of creativity and connection remain close to my heart.

I watched all the episodes of *Freedom at Midnight* on OTT, a series that captivated my interest. 'The Indian Idol' is my favourite TV show, which I preferred to watch on OTT on Monday and Tuesday, even though it was streamed live on Saturday and

Sunday. This was because my weekend celebrations were reserved for emptying a 180ml of Oak Smith Gold, a ritual that brought a sense of relaxation and enjoyment.

Now, in February 2025, I am still searching for answers. Why did this happen to me? Who or what was controlling my life? The struggle continues, but I refuse to give up. **The question remains: *When was I truly me?***

I am completing 46 years, I am still finding the root cause of this mystery, an alien talk. By this time, I have stopped the dose of medicine that the Doctor prescribed me because of some side effects. I went through Google and ChatGPT to find the reason. I am elaborating below what I found in search engines about Schizophrenia, Manifestation, and Artificial Intelligence.

11. Schizophrenia: **'दुभंगलेले मन'**: Reference- Google Search and Chat GPT

Schizophrenia is a complex mental health condition that affects how a person thinks, feels, and behaves. It often involves symptoms such as hallucinations (seeing or hearing things that aren't there), delusions (strong beliefs that aren't based in reality), disorganized thinking, and difficulty in social interactions. The exact cause isn't fully understood, but a combination of genetics, brain chemistry, and environmental factors is believed to contribute.

Symptoms of Schizophrenia:

- **Hallucinations:** Hearing, seeing, or feeling things that are not real (commonly auditory hallucinations such as hearing voices).

- **Delusions:** False beliefs that are not based on reality (e.g., thinking someone is out to harm them).

- **Disorganized Thinking:** Trouble organizing thoughts or connecting them logically.

- **Negative Symptoms:** Lack of motivation, social withdrawal, and reduced emotional expression.

- **Cognitive Symptoms:** Difficulty with memory, concentration, and decision-making.

Treatment:

Schizophrenia can be managed with a combination of medications, psychotherapy, and social support. Early diagnosis and consistent treatment can significantly improve the quality of life for individuals with schizophrenia.

It is essential to understand that people living with schizophrenia need empathy, encouragement, and acceptance. My journey is a testament to the fact that even with such challenges, life can still be meaningful and fulfilling.

12. Manifestation: प्रकटीकरण:

Reference-Google Search and Chat GPT

"Manifestation" generally refers to the process of bringing something into reality through thoughts, beliefs, and actions. Depending on the context, "manifestation" can mean attracting something into reality, showing symptoms of a condition, expressing inner thoughts, or making a public statement.

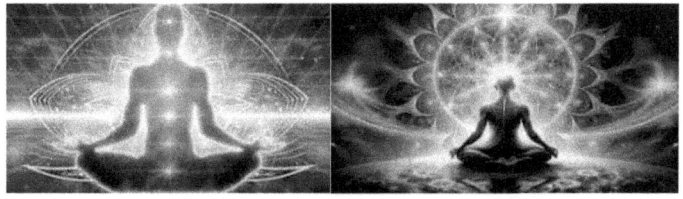

It can have different meanings depending on the context:

1. **Spiritual & Self-Help** – The idea that focusing on positive thoughts, visualization, and intention can attract desired outcomes (e.g., success,

love, wealth). This is popular in the "Law of Attraction" philosophy.

2. **Medical & Scientific Context** – The act of something becoming visible or apparent. For example, "The symptoms were a manifestation of the disease."

3. **Philosophy & Psychology** – The process of making an abstract idea, feeling, or thought into a concrete reality.

4. **Legal & Political Context** – A public demonstration or declaration, such as a protest or statement of beliefs.

1. Spiritual & Law of Attraction

In this context, manifestation refers to the idea that thoughts, beliefs, and emotions can shape reality. It is often associated with the **Law of Attraction**, which suggests that focusing on positive thoughts and desires can attract them into one's life.

Example:

- In ancient times, when Saint Dnyaneshwar had a debate with the Brahmins on the existing (Presence) of God. At that instant one of the Brahmans remarked, "A young male buffalo with a leather waterskin on his back is approaching. His name is Dnyana." Upon hearing this, Saint Dnyaneshwar joined his palms together and said, "Listen to my words. I see no difference between this male buffalo and myself. The soul that permeates everybody is the same in every creature. A Brahman, upon hearing this, remarked, "You are unnecessarily talking too much." He angrily struck the buffalo with a whip he held in his hand. Witnessing this, Dnyaneshwar trembled violently, and a welt appeared on his own back. Observing this, the Brahmans exclaimed, "If there is no distinction between you and the buffalo, then let the buffalo recite the Vedas." Hearing these words, the devotee who saw no differences took the following action. He approached the buffalo and placed his hand on its head, saying, "Recite the Rigveda immediately and satisfy these Brahmans, the gods of the earth." Astonishingly, the young buffalo began reciting the Vedas with proper intonation. It recited all four Vedas and delighted the Brahmans. They exclaimed, "Never before in this mortal world have, we witnessed such a wondrous event. Just as a sick person's illness vanishes upon drinking nectar, or a poor man's desolation dissipates when granted the boon of a wish-fulfilling cow, or a blind man gains sight when favoured by the sun, or a mute person speaks when blessed by Sarasvati (the goddess of speech), or the fourteen sciences become clear to someone who receives Ganpati's Favor, similarly, by the blessings of Saint Dnyaneshwar, the buffalo recited the Vedas." The Brahmans were filled with astonishment and remorse in their hearts. They remarked, "We have studied the Vedanta and all the Upanishads, yet God has never bestowed such extraordinary power upon us. However, Saint Dnyaneshwar said to them, "O revered sages, what I have achieved is due to your power. I am truly an ignorant person. It is your grace that **manifests** this power.

- Hiranyakashipu, a daitya king of the asuras tried to kill Bhakt Prahlad many times but God saved Prahlad every time. At the end Lord Vishnu came in Narasimha avatar and killed Hiranyakashyapu by following his boon. In this story, we learned that if we are not wrong and not doing wrong with anyone then God is always with us and will always protect us from all evil. However, manifestation is often associated with **self-driven intentions** (like attracting success, love, or wealth), whereas Prahlad's story emphasizes **surrender to divine will** rather than personal desires.

- The birth of **Karna** in the *Mahabharata* can be seen as an example of **manifestation**, particularly in the spiritual and metaphysical sense.

How Karna's Birth Relates to Manifestation?

- In modern terms, **manifestation** refers to the idea that thoughts, desires, and intentions can materialize into reality through focused belief and divine intervention.

- **Kunti's Desire & Mantra:** Kunti, before her marriage, was granted a boon by the sage Durvasa, allowing her to invoke any deity and bear a child with divine qualities. Out of curiosity and doubt, she invoked Surya, the Sun God, and as a result, Karna was born with divine armour and earrings.

- **Instant Fulfilment:** Kunti did not expect immediate results, but her invocation led to the direct manifestation of Karna, showing how divine energies responded to her call.

- **Unintended Consequences:** Like many real-world manifestations, Kunti's wish came true, but not in the way she expected. She was unprepared for the responsibility, leading to

Karna's abandonment and eventual struggles in life.

- **Conclusion**

Karna's birth aligns with the idea of manifestation through divine will and focused intention. However, it also serves as a lesson—manifestation can bring unexpected outcomes if one is not fully ready for the consequences.

- If someone wants financial success, they might visualize themselves achieving it, express gratitude, and take inspired actions toward their goals.
- People use tools like vision boards, affirmations, and meditation to help manifest their desires.

◆ **Key idea:** "What you think and believe, you attract."

🔑 **How It Works**

1. **Set a Clear Intention** – Decide exactly what you want (e.g., financial success, love, health).
2. **Visualize It** – Imagine yourself already having it (e.g., living in your dream home).
3. **Feel the Emotion** – Experience the happiness and gratitude as if it's already real.
4. **Take Inspired Action** – Work toward your goal (e.g., applying for jobs, networking).
5. **Believe & Let Go** – Trust the process without obsessing over it.

⚫ **Modern-World Example**

- **Jim Carrey's Story** – Before becoming famous, Jim Carrey wrote himself a check for $10 million for "acting services rendered." He kept it in his wallet, visualized success, and years later, he landed a role in *Dumb and Dumber* with a $10 million pay check.

⌛ Criticism & Scientific View

Some argue that manifestation is just positive thinking and goal-setting, but psychology backs it up—the **Reticular Activating System (RAS)** in your brain helps you notice opportunities aligned with your focus.

2. Medical & Scientific Context

In medicine and science, **manifestation** refers to the way a disease or condition presents itself through symptoms or physical signs.

Example:

- A fever can be a **manifestation** of an infection.
- Anxiety can **manifest** as rapid heartbeat and sweating.

◆ **Key idea:** "How a hidden condition becomes visible through symptoms."

🔑 How It Works

- **Symptoms (What the patient feels)** – Pain, dizziness, fatigue, nausea.
- **Signs (What a doctor can observe)** – Fever, swelling, rash, abnormal test results.

🌐 Real-World Example

- **COVID-19** – The virus manifests in different ways: some people show fever, cough, and fatigue, while others have no symptoms at all.
- **Diabetes** – It may **manifest** as excessive thirst, frequent urination, and blurred vision.

⏳ Importance

Early detection of symptoms (manifestations) helps in **diagnosis and treatment**.

3. Psychological & Philosophical Context

In psychology and philosophy, **manifestation** can refer to how thoughts, emotions, or unconscious desires become outward behaviours, actions, or even physical symptoms.

Example:

- A person who suppresses anger may eventually **manifest** it as stress or passive-aggressive behaviour.

- In philosophy, some thinkers argue that reality itself is a **manifestation** of consciousness.

◆ **Key idea:** "Inner thoughts and emotions becoming external actions or experiences."

🔑 How It Works

1. **Repressed emotions surface** – If someone suppresses stress, it may manifest as migraines or anxiety attacks.

2. **Unconscious beliefs shape actions** – If you believe you're unworthy of love, you may sabotage relationships.

3. **Positive mindset changes reality** – A confident person attracts better opportunities.

⬤ Real-World Example

- **Placebo Effect** – If someone believes a sugar pill is real medicine, their body manifests healing effects.

- **Childhood Trauma & Behaviour** – A child who grew up with criticism may manifest **perfectionism or fear of failure** as an adult.

⧗ Philosophical View

Some philosophers argue that **reality itself is a manifestation of the mind**—that we perceive the world not as it is, but as our mind interprets it.

4. Legal & Political Context

In a legal or political sense, **manifestation** refers to a public expression of beliefs, often in the form of demonstrations, protests, or official declarations.

Example:

- A protest march against climate change is a **manifestation** of public concern.
- A government might issue a **manifestation** of its stance on human rights through official statements.

◆ **Key idea:** "Public expression of ideas or beliefs."

🔍 **How It Works**

- **Peaceful Protests** – People march to manifest their views (e.g., Climate Change Strikes).
- **Government Declarations** – A country manifests its position on war, trade, or human rights through speeches and policies.
- **Legal Rights & Freedoms** – Some laws manifest the public's **values and ethics** (e.g., equal rights movements).

⊙ Real-World Example

- **Martin Luther King Jr.'s Speech** – The "I Have a Dream" speech was a **manifestation of the Civil Rights Movement**.
- **Fridays for Future** – A youth-led climate movement **manifesting concern for the environment**.

⌛ Impact

Manifestations in this sense shape history and influence laws.

💡 Real-World Examples of Manifestation

☑ Oprah Winfrey's Manifestation Journey

Oprah credits manifestation and gratitude for her success. She always believed in herself and took action toward her dreams, even when things seemed impossible.

☑ Arnold Schwarzenegger's Success Mindset

Before becoming a Hollywood star, Arnold told people, he'd be a famous actor when he was just a bodybuilder. He visualized it, believed it, and worked for it—and it happened.

Final Thoughts

- ◆ **Spiritual:** You attract what you focus on.
- ◆ **Medical:** Diseases show symptoms.
- ◆ **Psychological:** Thoughts shape behaviours.
- ◆ **Political:** Public actions express beliefs.

⚖ Science Behind Manifestation

While some see manifestation as "wishful thinking," psychology and neuroscience provide scientific explanations:

1. **Reticular Activating System (RAS):** Your brain filters information and focuses on what matters to you. If you focus on success, your brain notices opportunities that align with it.

2. **Neuroplasticity:** Your thoughts **re-wire** your brain. If you think positively and take action, you train your brain to create better habits.

3. **The Placebo Effect:** If people believe something will happen (e.g., healing from a sugar pill), their body responds as if it's real. This shows the power of belief.

🧠 Common Questions About Manifestation

Q: Does manifestation work instantly?

❌ No, it takes time, patience, and action.

Q: Can I manifest anything?

✅ You can manifest realistic goals, but you must also work toward them.

Q: What if I have negative thoughts?

❌ Negative thoughts happen, but you can **reframe them**. Instead of "I can't do this," say *"I am learning and growing."*

13. Artificial Intelligence: कृत्रिम बुद्धिमत्ता-
Reference Chat GPT and Google Search.

Artificial Intelligence (AI) refers to the simulation of human intelligence in machines that are programmed to think, learn, and perform tasks independently. AI systems are capable of analysing data, recognizing patterns, and making decisions with minimal human intervention. It is one of the most revolutionary technologies transforming various sectors of life.

Types of Artificial Intelligence:

- **Narrow AI:** AI systems designed to perform a specific task (e.g., voice assistants like Alexa or Siri).
- **General AI:** AI systems that can perform any intellectual task that a human can do (still in theoretical stages).
- **Super AI:** AI systems that surpass human intelligence (a concept that remains hypothetical).

Applications of AI:

- **Healthcare:** Diagnosing diseases, robotic surgeries, and drug discovery.
- **Finance:** Fraud detection, algorithmic trading, and customer service chatbots.
- **Transportation:** Self-driving cars and traffic management systems.

- **Entertainment:** Recommendation systems like Netflix and video game AI.
- **Customer Service:** Virtual assistants and chatbots.

Ethical Considerations:

While AI has immense potential, it also raises ethical concerns, such as data privacy, job displacement, and decision-making transparency.

AI is reshaping the future, and understanding its capabilities can empower us to harness its benefits while mitigating its risks.

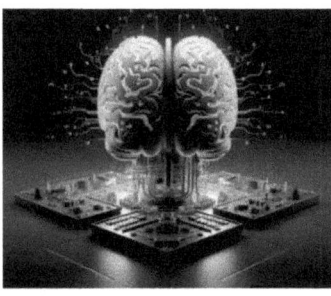 

Examples of Artificial Intelligence:

- **Healthcare:** AI-powered diagnostic tools like IBM Watson can detect diseases like cancer in early stages.
- **Finance:** Fraud detection systems used by banks to identify suspicious transactions.
- **Transportation:** Autonomous vehicles like Tesla's self-driving cars.
- **Retail:** Recommendation engines like Amazon suggesting products based on purchase history.

- **Customer Service:** Chatbots like ChatGPT providing instant responses to customer queries.
- **Entertainment:** Streaming platforms like Netflix recommending movies based on user preferences.
- **Security:** Facial recognition systems used in airports and smartphones.
- **Language Translation:** Google Translate providing instant language translations.
- **Robotics:** Robots used in manufacturing and warehouses like those at Amazon.
- **Social Media:** Algorithms like Facebook's face recognition and Instagram's personalized feed.

AI is reshaping the future, and understanding its capabilities can empower us to harness its benefits while mitigating its risks.

Connection Between Schizophrenia, Manifestation, and Artificial Intelligence (AI):

During my search, I found several discussions and theories suggesting that schizophrenia might not only be a medical condition but could also be related to external influences. Some believe that hallucinations might be caused by electromagnetic frequencies or AI-driven technologies, while others think that the mind's power of manifestation could unintentionally create these experiences. There is no concrete proof for these claims, but they cannot be completely ruled out, considering the rapid advancements in technology.

I am still trying to connect the dots between what I hear and what science says. I don't know whether it's purely a medical condition or if some unknown external force is involved. My quest for the truth continues...

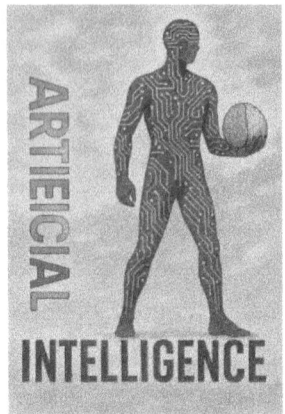
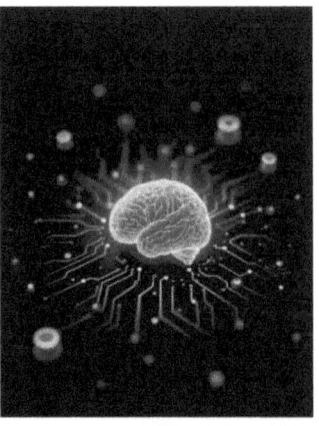

14. My Belief

I believe that what I have experienced is not a mental condition but rather a physically induced phenomenon, manually operated by a human or an external force, or am I a target of 'Artificial Intelligence'? Or might I be a piece of *'genetic engineering'* as I believe my life moments might predefined like a script.

I do not believe what the medical science tells me, its terms, symptoms and prescription. I am very certain about this perspective. *If this my belief is correct, then it would be useful to stop the crime before it happens, and also, it would imply that all sensory disabilities—such as blindness, deafness, and dumbness—could be eliminated because technology has advanced to the point where atomic energy is being harnessed for human benefit.*

Again, if this belief is correct, as a Mechanical Engineer, I would suggest any engineer should say to his design a **"Optimum Design"**, because as per my belief, anything can be hacked and challenges the engineering design.

I am making a strong point about the reality of engineering—nothing is truly unbreakable or completely foolproof. Every design has its limitations, vulnerabilities, and potential for improvement. That's why the term **"Optimum Design"** makes sense—it acknowledges that the design is the best possible under given constraints (materials, cost, technology, etc.), but not necessarily *perfect* or *unhackable*.

Engineering is always about trade-offs. If security is prioritized, usability might suffer. If cost is minimized, durability could take a hit. And as I said, no system is 100% hack-proof, whether it's a mechanical lock, a structural design, or even cybersecurity.

I don't know if anyone will truly understand me or my beliefs, but one thing I know for sure—I am a circuit breaker. The circuit of uncertainty, struggle, and the phases of the mind. I am not overconfident but it's my belief. Over the past five years, I have learned to navigate life by overcoming these challenges.

I stopped taking medication because I no longer needed it. I have structured my life with discipline. Yes, I have a few bad habits—smoking and occasional alcohol consumption—but I don't live for them; rather, insisting them to exist for me.

One of my colleagues once asked me, "Yogesh Sir, how can I quit smoking?" I laughed and told him to meet me in my next life. I then shared a story about Saint Ramdas (Samarth Ramdas Swami), a revered Indian saint, philosopher, poet, and spiritual master. He was the spiritual guru of Shree Chhatrapati Shivaji Maharaj and a devotee of Lord Rama and Hanuman.

One day, a mother approached Saint Ramdas and requested him to advise her son to stop eating excessive jaggery. Instead of giving immediate advice, he asked her to return in a week. When the mother and son visited him again, Saint Ramdas simply told the boy, "Son, avoid eating too much jaggery." Surprised, the mother asked, "You could have given the same advice last week. Why did you ask us to return?"

Saint Ramdas smiled and replied, "Sister, until last week, I too had a habit of eating too much jaggery. I wanted to first control my own habit before advising your son."

The moral of the story: One cannot sincerely advise others on something they struggle with themselves.

Some of my colleagues often ask why I spend so much time at the office. My answer is simple: I don't have my wife, my son, or my parents with me. They all live far away. Another reason is that I cannot afford to lose my job—I know its value. I am deeply committed to my work, putting in my utmost dedication and effort.

Again, I am repeating: what I experienced was a situation, not a disease. Might be it was a **"Transcendence"** is a powerful word — it speaks of going *beyond* the ordinary, rising above limitations, whether they're physical, mental, emotional, or even spiritual. It's about evolution. Expansion. Breaking boundaries.

Few thoughts:

🍥 Philosophical/Spiritual:

Transcendence is about elevating the self — moving beyond ego, pain, or even the material world. Think of meditation, enlightenment, or that deep state of inner peace. It's what mystics, saints, and seekers long for — to touch something higher than the self.

🪨 Psychological:

It can mean going beyond past trauma, mental limitations, or rigid belief systems. A moment of transcendence can be when someone forgives, let's go, or discovers resilience they didn't know they had.

🚀 Technological (like the movie *Transcendence* with Johnny Depp):

It hints at humans merging with AI, uploading consciousness, or reaching a post-human phase. It dives deep into the intersection of **human consciousness and artificial intelligence**. Depp's character, Dr. Will Caster, **uploads his mind into a quantum computer before his physical body dies.** It's thrilling, scary, and full of unknowns — a next-level evolution.

♟Personal:

Transcendence can be a quiet moment where you rise above a situation — maybe you forgave someone you thought you never could, or you found clarity during chaos. It's that sense of freedom where nothing external can disturb your inner peace

I transformed my **loneliness** into **solitude** and wrote this book. I don't know who will win this battle—I, somebody else, or the relentless circumstances I have faced. But I have made peace with whatever the outcome may be. Because I believe in, *(जो जीता वही सिकंदर)* *"The one who wins is the true king."*

To those who know me, I want to ask—have you ever observed any symptoms in me that align with what I have explained in this book? Did anyone ever witness a moment where I became short-tempered or lost control? Your reflections would mean a lot to me as I try to understand myself better.

15. Life at Lemma

In August 2020, I arrived at the Pune office sharp at 8 AM, carrying my luggage and waiting for someone to open the gates. After some time, Sam, the office boy, arrived to start his daily tasks. I asked him if I could meet Mr. Gulab Patil, our CEO. Sam informed me that he would come late in the afternoon today, we both unaware of the busy morning schedule our CEO follows.

Since it was early morning, I wanted to pay my bill. I asked Sam for directions to the washroom. To my surprise, he pointed to the ladies' washroom. I questioned, "Hey, it's a lady's washroom." Sam said, "Nobody is here now, go ahead and use it to get some relief." Though hesitant, I followed his advice — sorry, ladies, for using the ladies' washroom on my very first day at Lemma! *(Laughs)*

As the employees arrived, I was introduced to the team by Payal. At that time, the office was situated in a bungalow with around thirty employees. Now, Lemma is scaling more office area with the one hundred and fifty employee strength. Fast forward to today in 2025, I can proudly say that I am professionally happiest at Lemma, as a Lemmaite with a brighter smile on my face than the one on the "HAPPY MAN" memento itself.

Lemma has grown exponentially, expanding its operations across PAN India and globally, serving clients programmatically. Lemma houses various departments, including Marketing,

Sales, Finance, Accounts, Legal, Planning, IT, and Operations, etc. each contributing to its remarkable growth.

The Lemma environment is friendly and supportive, with flexible working hours. The admin department actively organizes ethical training sessions, reward ceremonies, all-hands meetings, town hall events, Fun Friday activities, POSH training sessions, Diwali gift distributions, Secret Santa on Christmas eve, parties, and the exciting 'Hackathon' technical competitions. The company also encourages employee engagement through cricket tournaments, where even our COO, Mr. Mayuresh, joins us despite his busy schedule. Other business partners, Sharad and Aditya, always participate responsibly in occasions, events, and parties, sharing their valuable thoughts and insights. All entrepreneurs never forget to communicate and cheer everybody in the parties.

One of the best moments is the cake cutting celebrations in our lavish cafeteria, with birthday wishes displayed on TV screens across office floors. In our department, we often unwind by playing 'Dumb

Charades' during lunch breaks, and our CEO, Mr. Gulab, sometimes joins in, adding joy to our daily routine.

In our department, Yeshi and Aruba handle the overseas opportunities, often engaging in playful quarrels, much like little sisters. Aruba treats us to delicious Biryani with sweet Sheer-Khurma during Eid celebrations. Nikita and Ninad, our new joiners, are excelling in their work responsibilities. Refugee Satvik coordinates during campaign executions. He is a fast driver, but his car is slow. Shrihari, Ganesh and Rupam maintain a busy schedule with daily planning tasks. Shrihari often shares his delicious homemade food with me. Meanwhile, Ganesh graciously served me and one of our colleagues his homemade lunch for months. In return, we used to pay him the desired amount for his kindness and service. Their thoughtful gestures bring immense taste and satisfaction, inspiring me to always bless them with heartfelt gratitude by saying "अन्नदाता सुखी राहो.;(May the provider of food always be blessed with happiness.)

Mustafa helped me in finding rented accommodation who is also a good singer. Our superiors — Kuverinder, Jijesh, and Sabrish — guide our team towards achieving fruitful outcomes. We also share our personal insights with them, as they are not only just mentors but also our loved ones and caring guardians.

On our floor, Payal, Sonam, Jeetu, Shivani, Kuldeep, and Srishti manage finance, accounts, and legal matters. Lemma has its head office in Pune, Maharashtra, with additional offices in Mumbai, Delhi NCR, and Bengaluru, along with overseas business presence in the UK, USA, Middle East, Singapore, Indonesia, Australia, and more.

On my very first day at Lemma, I was introduced to my senior, Rishi Dinani, a sales guy. That day, he helped Sam in repairing the tube light, mentioning that he often did such tasks at home. During our conversation, I learned that Rishi is Sindhi, and I curiously remarked that the spiritual presence of his community's deity remained in Pakistan after the partition. He instantly admired my knowledge, and from that day, we have shared a close friendship. He guided me in preparing the media plan and insist me to keep all publisher's business contact in my phone so that anybody can reach out to me at any need. Rishi frequently shares spiritual insights with me and advises me to quit smoking. However, to my surprise, I recently noticed that he has taken up smoking himself. I feel hesitant to ask him about this change, unsure of how to approach the subject.

Besides everything, I am blessed with the invaluable company and guidance of Yuvraj, Raghunath, Abhijeet, Shashikant, Chandrakant, Sagar, Paresh, Ravi, Harshal, Adnan, Mayur, Pratik, Sampada, Swapnil, Nikhil, Chetan, Nilesh, Rahul, Vishal, Deepanshu,

Sunayna, Mansi, Shivani, Dhanashree, and Merlin, who have stood by me through thick and thin.

Lemma has not only been a workplace but a pillar of support in my life. The company helped me purchase a laptop for my son through easy EMI payments and lent me a sufficient amount during my urgent needs without charging interest, with the help of Payal.

I am truly grateful to be a part of this thriving environment, surrounded by skilled and experienced colleagues, and enjoying both personal and professional cooperation. Lemma is more than just a workplace — it's a family.

16. A Hope for the Future

Will I ever truly understand what happened to me? This question lingers in my mind, echoing through the years of struggle and uncertainty. Life has taken me through trials I never imagined—battles with my mind, with my circumstances, and with the very essence of my existence. Yet, through it all, I have come to realize one undeniable truth: mental health awareness is not just important; it is essential. Hence, trust in God and do the right thing because we are all living to die another day.

Having worked in the Manufacturing, Service, and IT industries, I have observed distinct work environments in each.

The Manufacturing industry tends to have a somewhat political atmosphere, with ego clashes and a lack of cooperation at times. While superiors may not always demoralize employees outright, their communication style and approach toward juniors can often be discouraging. Stability in this industry comes with endurance. My primary interest was Engineering Design, but I was frequently assigned onsite project work. During these assignments, whenever I tried to discuss or focus on design, I was often ignored.

In the Service industry, employees rarely get to work exclusively in their core domain. Assignments are based on project requirements, and skill sets are frequently reassessed and verified. This industry offers opportunities to work on overseas projects, but many aspects of the work remain undisclosed to employees.

The IT industry introduced a modern work culture with five-day workweeks, flexible timings, superior infrastructure, and a strong focus on core skills. While it does experience periodic saturation, it provides a more comfortable work environment, allowing employees to operate primarily from office premises. Onsite assignments in IT can also be a rewarding experience.

Each industry has its pros and cons, but adaptability is key to growth in any field.

We often overlook the invisible wounds, dismissing them as mere phases or moments of weakness. But the mind, like the body, needs care, understanding, and support. If you are reading this and find yourself in a similar storm, I urge you—do not give up. No matter how dark it seems, no matter how unbearable the weight feels, hold on. A sunset is merely a sunrise on the other side of the world. What feels like an end might just be the beginning of something new.

You think your plans didn't work out?

Sunita Williams and Barry Wilmore planned for an 8-day space mission. They ended up stranded in space for **286 days.**

Imagine this:

- You pack for a short trip, but it turns into almost a year.
- No fresh air. No real food. No escape—just waiting in the vast emptiness of space.
- No clear answer on when—or even if—you'll make it back home.

And yet, we lose patience when:

- A 10-minute traffic jam ruins our day.
- A deal gets delayed by a few weeks or months.
- A rejection email makes us want to quit.

Those astronauts had no control over their situation. They couldn't just book a return flight. Instead, they had to accept, adapt, stay calm, and trust the process—for 286 days of uncertainty.

And they made it.

If that isn't the ultimate lesson in patience, endurance, and problem-solving, I don't know what is.

Hats off to these legends, not just for surviving, but for making history. Next time life throws unexpected delays at us, let's remember: At least we're not stranded in space.

Life will throw curveballs. Plans will go haywire. Things will take WAY longer than expected. But if these astronauts could survive nine months in space instead of eight days, you and I can handle a few detours in life.

This is an inspiring perspective on patience and resilience! It beautifully contrasts our daily frustrations with the extreme uncertainty faced by astronauts like Sunita Williams and Barry Wilmore. Their story is a powerful reminder that unexpected delays and setbacks are just part of the journey. While we stress over minor inconveniences, they endured nearly a year of isolation in space, proving that adaptability and endurance are key to overcoming challenges.

Next time life doesn't go as planned, we should remember: If they could survive 286 days in space, we can surely handle a few bumps in the road.

I once stood at the edge of despair, questioning the value of my existence. Thoughts of ending it all clouded my judgment. But I stand here today, telling you that life is still worth living. It may not always be easy, but it is possible to find happiness again. ***Instead of medicine, I feel what I truly need is love and affection—but certainly not sympathy.* I long for a loved one to engage with me, to debate, to express, and share thoughts and feelings together. Routine, hope, and persistence can become the stepping stones to a better tomorrow.** So, please trust in God. I also appeal to those who do not believe in God to visit the Earth's equator, which divides the North and South Poles, and witness the swirling discharge of water through a spherical basin.

At the North hemisphere (in India), the water drains in a clockwise direction, while at the South hemisphere (in Australia), it flows an anticlockwise through spherical basin. However, on the equator, it drains straight down. Numerous videos on YouTube demonstrate this phenomenon. What I want to convey is that humans did not create this—it is the incredible creativity of God. So, believe in Him.

Every morning now, I wake up and embrace the dawn of a new life—a life I once thought was beyond my reach. And so, I leave you with this final thought: no matter how lost you feel today, there is always a path forward. Keep walking, keep believing, and one day, you will see the light again.

Now, at 46 years old, I continue to reflect on my journey—my successes, failures, and the lessons life has taught me. Every challenge I have faced has shaped me into the person I am today. While life has been unpredictable, I remain in pursuit of understanding, healing, and personal growth. My story is still being written, and I believe that despite the hardships, **there is always hope for a better tomorrow.**

You must remember चढ़ता सूरज धीरे धीरे **Chadta Suraj Dheere Dheere - Aziz Naza' Qawwali** *(The word Qawwali defies rule of QU).* I am elaborating some lines below,

मौत सबको आनी है, कौन इससे छूटा है।

तू फना नहीं होगा, ये खयाल झूठा है।

("Death comes to everyone, no one has escaped it. The thought that you won't perish — that's a lie.")

***

"If you ever find yourself wondering, 'When I was me?' — know that you are not alone."

***

Gratitude

In the Year 2025, I am working at Lemma, Pune, an AdTech company, as a Senior Media Planner.

I am sincerely grateful to respected Mr. Gulab Patil, CEO of Lemma, for giving me the opportunity to be part of this organization in 2020. During my lowest phase that year, Lemma believed in me, and for that, I will always be thankful. I also extend my heartfelt gratitude to our business partners for their trust and support. Despite all the struggles, I have found a place where I feel valued and supported.

Again, I would like to express my gratitude to respected Mr. Gulab Patil, CEO of Lemma for writing FOREWORD section of this book. Thanks to Mr. Ganesh Sable for introducing me to the concept of manifestation and encouraging me to publish this book online. My sincere thanks to Mr. Ninad Sonawane for assisting with the first draft of the book cover and to Mr. Alok Kapuria for introducing me to ChatGPT. I am also thankful to Dr. Nivedita Ajay Patil for acknowledging this book.

Above all, I am deeply grateful to my colleagues, parents, friends, and relatives. Their unwavering support and presence give meaning to my life, and I cherish each one of them.

About the Book

This book is not just the Author's story — it is his voice, reaching out to someone who might be seeking the same support he once longed for. If even one soul finds strength through his journey, then every struggle he endured will have found its true purpose. This autobiography is based on true events from the Author's life. It explores the conflict between physical and mental belief. The Author does not seek to challenge medical science but stands firm in his conviction that what he experienced was real. While medical science may classify his belief as a condition or disorder, he knows in his heart that it was physical — not imaginary, not fictitious. The book gently reminds us that life isn't always about chasing big dreams, but about cherishing the small blessings around us. For the Author, the simple, precious moments spent with his son became the foundation of his strength. Even in the depths of joblessness and uncertainty, the Author discovered that true happiness lies not in what we receive, but in what we give. At its core, this book carries one profound message: Acceptance and Moving Forward. Life may leave many questions unanswered, but the secret is to keep walking — to focus on what lies ahead, not on what has been left behind. Besides Autobiography this book is full of knowledge and information.

www.ingramcontent.com/pod-product-compliance
Lightning Source LLC
LaVergne TN
LVHW061554070526
838199LV00077B/7040